Creative Stained Glass

Modern Designs & Simple Techniques

Creative Stained Glass

Modern Designs & Simple Techniques

Christine Kellmann Stevenson

LARK BOOKS
A Division of Sterling Publishing Co., Inc.
New York

DEDICATION

Thank you to my parents,
Dorothy and Russell,
for giving me wings. Thanks to
my husband and partner, Ed,
for encouraging me to fly.

EDITOR
Katherine Duncan Aimone

ART DIRECTOR
Susan McBride

COVER DESIGN
Barbara Zaretsky

ASSOCIATE ART DIRECTOR
Shannon Yokeley

ASSISTANT EDITORS
Nathalie Mornu
Rebecca Lim

EDITORIAL ASSISTANCE
Delores Gosnell

PHOTOGRAPHY
Keith Wright
keithwright.com

ILLUSTRATION
Orrin Lundgren

The Library of Congress has cataloged the hardcover edition as follows:

Stevenson, Christine Kellmann.
  Creative stained glass : modern designs & simple techniques /
Christine Kellmann Stevenson.
    p. cm.
  ISBN 1-57990-487-4 (hardcover)
  1. Glass craft. 2. Glass painting and staining. I. Title.
TT298.S73 2004
748.5--dc22

2003024958

10 9 8 7 6 5 4 3 2 1

Published by Lark Books, a division of
Sterling Publishing Co., Inc.
387 Park Avenue South, New York, N.Y. 10016

First Paperback Edition 2007
© 2004, Christine Kellmann Stevenson

Distributed in Canada by Sterling Publishing,
c/o Canadian Manda Group, 165 Dufferin Street
Toronto, Ontario, Canada M6K 3H6

Distributed in the United Kingdom by GMC Distribution Services,
Castle Place, 166 High Street, Lewes, East Sussex, England BN7 1XU

Distributed in Australia by Capricorn Link (Australia) Pty Ltd.,
P.O. Box 704, Windsor, NSW 2756 Australia

If you have questions or comments about this book, please contact:
Lark Books
67 Broadway
Asheville, NC 28801
(828) 253-0467

Manufactured in China

ISBN 13: 978-1-57990-487-6 (hardcover) 978-1-60059-132-7 (paperback)
ISBN 10: 1-57990-487-4 (hardcover) 1-60059-132-9 (paperback)

For information about custom editions, special sales, premium and corporate purchases, please
contact Sterling Special Sales Department at 800-805-5489 or specialsales@sterlingpub.com.

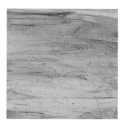

Table *of* Contents

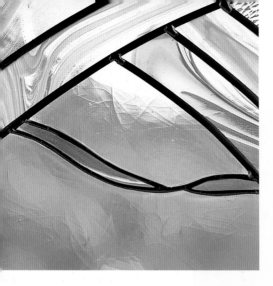

Introduction

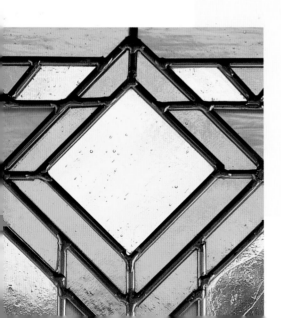

Working with stained glass is more popular and accessible to all of us than it ever has been. It's amazing how simple pieces of glass, held together by lead or soldered foil, can be combined to produce pieces that are magical when lighted. The effects of stained glass can be calming, energizing, and incredibly seductive. First used for devotional purposes in religious settings, this art has now grown into an industry of professionals and hobbyists who make pieces for homes, offices, and other architectural settings.

Twenty years of teaching, combined with my experience of running a retail stained glass business, has allowed me to develop methods for making projects that are fun, easy, and as economical as possible. With practice and patience, you'll reap the incredible rewards that this art has to offer. I'm confident, too, that

the fascinating properties of glass will lure you into your studio or workspace to spend many satisfying hours creating stained glass projects.

This book begins at the beginning: You'll learn everything you need to know about how to safely undertake the creation of your first pieces. If you have worked with stained glass before, then you'll be inspired by innovative designs that take advantage of the many glass choices available on the market. You'll build on your knowledge by learning more advanced techniques as well.

And, today's helpful and efficient tools make working with glass easier than ever before. All the basics of how to use these tools are covered—from making patterns from the templates provided, to safely cutting the glass, to carefully assembling and soldering pieces together.

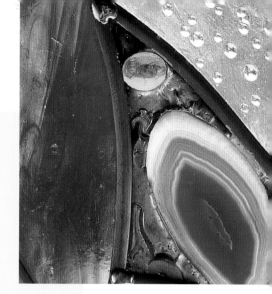

How-to photos guide you gently through leading and copper foiling (the two assembly techniques used for stained glass). You'll also learn how to combine these two techniques for a different look. In addition, you'll be introduced to techniques such as incorporating natural geodes or glass nuggets as well as using patinas and overlay pieces to further enhance your work.

Then, after you've digested the basics, 27 projects lead you step-by-step through making each one. The projects range from very simple to more complex, providing you with a wide range of both visual and technical choices. These designs are fresh from my studio, and their inspiration comes from sources as plain as doodles to references as sophisticated as photographs or paintings.

The proportions of most of the flat pieces are guided by their possible use as entry (door) side-lights, window panels, or cabinet doors. A clever window transom can be used between cabinets or over a window. Regardless, all projects can be equipped with hanging devices that allow them to be displayed in front of existing windows without the need to install them. You'll also learn how to make a basic flat fan lamp and a traditional four-sided lamp. Another eye-catching project shows you how to combine stained glass and a piece of cut mirrored glass.

It is my hope that you'll fall in love with this craft the way that I did many years ago. If you've thought of taking up stained glass but have never followed through, this book is your answer. Begin today!

Christine Kellmann Stevenson

Stained Glass Basics

The following sections will give you a thorough overview of the glass, materials, supplies, tools, and equipment that you'll be working with as you create stained glass pieces. Read through them to familiarize yourself with each item, and then use them as a reference for purchasing items from a stained glass supplier.

Types of Stained Glass

Even before being cut and pieced together into a project, the sheer beauty of stained glass is magical. So many colors, textures, and types are available that you may feel thrilled and overwhelmed at the same time! But don't fear, the following section will help you sort through the main types and give you a working knowledge.

At the beginning of each project, you'll find a list of the types of glass used to create the particular piece. Even though we suggest glass combinations, you may want to come up with your own color schemes.

In general, stained glass falls into two main categories: cathedral and opalescent (or opals). Cathedral glass is the category of all clear and transparent colored glass. By contrast, opalescent glass is made with a material that causes the glass to crystallize during the cooling process, resulting in glass with varying degrees of opaqueness that reflects light rather than transmitting it.

There are many variations within the categories of cathedral and opalescent. Some of the more common types are described below. Keep in mind that terminology varies from region to region, and even from studio to studio. So don't be alarmed if your local retailer or a glass catalogue refers to what you're looking for by another name. Based on the photos of the projects in this book, you should still be able to find something very close to what we've used.

Many of the glass types that you'll discover are combinations of various types, such as hammered iridescent cathedral glass or glue-chip bevels. Glass manufacturers are constantly developing new and exciting combinations to keep the ever-evolving field of stained glass alive.

In addition, found objects such as geodes, seashells, marbles, glass tiles, or any object that can be copper-foiled or leaded can be used to enhance and complement the different kinds of glass in your project.

Antique glass

Made to look like it's old, the machine-made version of this glass has a slightly distorted texture while being even in color and thickness. Mouth-blown antique glass is made using a technique that results in distortions, some bubbles, and variations in color intensity within individual sheets.

Bevels

These thick, flat, precut glass shapes have been machine-beveled to an angle. Bevels act as prisms, refracting the light that passes through them into a rainbow of colors. They are available in a number of geometric shapes as well as groupings, called clusters. They are usually clear (cathedral) or may be glue-chipped (see below).

Glue-chip glass

This textured cathedral glass has been treated so that it resembles a frost-covered window. The name refers to the technique used to create the effect: Hot glue is applied to sandblasted glass, and, as it dries, the glue peels away flakes of glass, resulting in the pattern. Double glue-chipped glass has been treated twice to create a tighter texture.

Iridescent glass

This glass, which can be either cathedral or opalescent, has been thinly coated with metallic oxides to produce a colorful rainbow-like shimmer. The rainbow effect is more pronounced on darker colors of glass.

Hammered texture glass

This glass, which comes in both cathedral and opalescent, has a texture similar to that of hammered copper.

Glass nuggets

These small globs of glass are made by dropping hot glass on a flat surface. They are flat on the bottom and rounded on the top. Nuggets come in both cathedral and opalescent.

Ring-mottled glass

This opalescent glass is mottled with small, roughly circular patterns that are more opaque than the surrounding glass.

Ripple glass

This glass, which is either cathedral or opalescent, has a rippled texture. The effect varies from manufacturer to manufacturer, and various colors are available.

Rondels

These are mouth-blown glass pieces, spun into a flat circular shape much like the bottom of a bottle. They vary in size and shape and are usually transparent (cathedral).

Seedy glass

Usually of the cathedral variety, this glass derives its name from the seed-like bubbles trapped below the surface. (Note: When cutting this glass, you'll learn to "roll" over the bubbles as you score over them.)

Wispy glass

This glass is made by mixing cathedral glass with another more transparent color. However, the cathedral glass usually dominates.

Streaky glass

Glass made up of one or more cathedral colors mixed together with a white opalescent color to create a thinly streaked, multicolored glass. In this glass, the opalescent glass usually dominates.

Wavy glass

This popular glass has the appearance of a gently rippled lake. Combinations of both cathedral and opalescent are available.

Tools of the Trade

The following list, divided by usage, gives you an overview of tools and supplies used in this book. A well-stocked stained glass shop will carry most of the things that are made particularly for this craft. Detailed descriptions and how to use them follow in this chapter.

Don't be intimidated by the number of items. You can pick and choose from them as you learn and when you decide which projects you want to undertake. (Each project has a separate list of supplies you'll need to make it). Some of these things are so simple that they need no explanation—it's just a good idea to have them around. In fact, you may already have them in your house or garage.

Patterns & Glass Cutting
Materials & Supplies
- Permanent markers in black and white
- Carbon paper
- Heavyweight kraft paper
- Glass in various colors and patterns

Tools
- Pattern shears
- Scissors
- Glass cutter and cutting fluid
- Straightedge, triangle, and other tools for drawing lines
- Breaking pliers
- Running pliers
- Grozing pliers
- Glass grinder, face shield, coolant
- Carbide grinding stone
- Light table (optional)

Soldering

Materials & Supplies
- Solid-core 50/50 and 60/40 solder
- Flux (liquid, paste, or gel), flux brush, flux remover
- Sponge

Tools
- Soldering iron (900-1000°F [500-537°C]) and holder

Lead Work

Materials & Supplies
(specific to projects in this book)
- Lead came, H-channel: $7/32$ inch (5 mm) and $1/4$ inch (6 mm)
- Brass came, U-channel: $3/8$ inch (9.5 mm)
- Brass-capped lead came, H-channel: $7/32$ inch (5 mm)
- Zinc came, U-channel: $1/4$ (6 mm) and $3/8$ inch (9.5 mm)

Tools
- Lead vise
- Lead nippers (dykes)
- Hacksaw (handsaw) with metal cutting blade or small electric cutting saw (optional)
- Metal files
- Horseshoe nails (50 mm)
- Glazing hammer
- Wire brush
- Channel-lock pliers

Copper Foil Work

Materials & Supplies
(specific to projects in this book)
- Copper foil: $3/16$ inch (4 mm) and $7/32$ inch (5 mm) in regular, black, and silver-backed
- Copper reinforcing strip

Tools
- Crimper or burnisher
- Single-blade razorblade cutter

Finishing

Materials & Supplies
- Patinas
- Stained glass cement
- Whiting
- Cotton balls, lint-free paper towels or cotton rags, cotton-tipped swabs

Tools
- Natural-bristle hand brush

Display

Materials & Supplies
(specific to projects in this book):
- 18-gauge tinned wire
- 21-gauge copper wire
- Brass hangers
- Brass shim ($1/16$ inch [1.6 mm])
- Brass pin-back clips
- Jack chain

Tools
- Wire cutters
- Needle-nose pliers

Safety

Materials & Supplies
- Safety glasses
- Rubber gloves
- Shop apron
- Kitchen hot pad or oven glove
- "Thumb savers" and face shield for grinder

General Cleaning

Materials & Supplies
- Non-ammonia glass cleaner
- Lint-free towels

Tools
- Table brush
- Dustpan

Materials & Supplies

The following descriptions cover many items. You won't need all of them to begin working in stained glass, so you might want to purchase just what you need for a project. Later, as your interest and skill grows, you'll want to keep certain items stocked in your workspace.

Came

Came is grooved metal stripping that holds glass pieces together. It can be made from lead, brass-capped lead, zinc, brass, or copper. Solder is used to tack the joints together where the pieces meet.

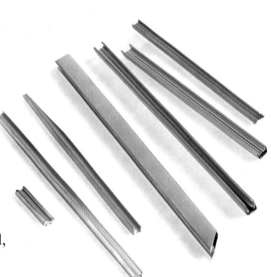

The most commonly used and durable came is made of lead. For this reason, all projects assembled with came are referred to as leaded, even if they're held together with other types of came.

Lead makes sense for stained glass, particularly outdoor pieces, because it resists corrosion by water and chemicals. It's also a wonderfully malleable metal, making it relatively easy to bend and shape around pieces of glass. Lead came is easy to cut with special lead nippers. On the other hand, this material's relative softness and malleability make it prone to sagging. To increase the rigidity of lead came, you have to stretch it before using it (see page 22).

Zinc, brass, or copper came is much harder than lead and has to be cut with a bladed hacksaw. Because these cames don't bend easily, they're used primarily for straight lines, such as panel borders or geometric designs without curves. Because it's strong and lightweight, zinc came is specified for the borders on most of the projects in this book.

SAFETY: The dangers of ingesting or inhaling lead or permitting it to enter your bloodstream can be serious. Keep it away from your food and from your animals and children. Wash your hands thoroughly every time you stop working with lead. Use a good cream or pumice hand-cleaner to remove as much lead as possible from your skin. Then follow up by washing with soap and water, scrubbing your fingernails thoroughly as you do. When you're through working for the day, take a shower, and wash your hair. To be certain that you don't inhale airborne particles from lead, you can wear a tight-fitting dust mask. In general, use common sense and limit your exposure by taking a few simple precautions. Lead is a wonderful and effective material to use for stained glass, but you must respect its potential hazards.

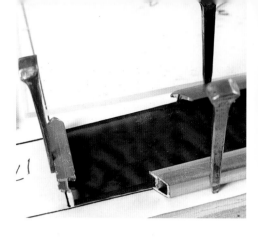

Bumpers

These are scrap pieces of came left over from assembling a panel that you can use to hold the glass pieces in place while you construct a panel with came of the same size. Because they're the same height and width, they show you how far the final pieces of came will overlap the glass. This will allow you to accurately measure and cut the came pieces so that you can replace them as you assemble (see pages 36-39).

Copper foil

When making projects from smaller, intricate pieces, it's better to join them using copper foil and solder. Adhesive-backed copper foil, sold in 36-yard (32.4 m) rolls, is wrapped around the smooth, ground edges of each piece of glass. The foil serves as a base for the solder to hold the glass together.

Copper foil comes in several sizes, but 3/16- and 7/32-inch (5 and 5.5 cm) widths are the most common. Since it will show through the glass, the adhesive backing is made in copper, silver, or black. For instance, if you plan to apply a black patina to your finished project (see page 16), be sure to use black-backed foil on clear or light-colored glass. Likewise, if you plan to leave the solder its natural silver color, you'll probably want to use a silver-backed foil.

You can buy a dispenser for your copper foil that makes it easier to handle. Regardless, always store your foil in an airtight bag or container when not in use to prevent oxidation.

Copper reinforcing strip (re-strip)

A thicker, sturdier strip of copper can be inserted between copper-foiled pieces of glass before the seams of the project are soldered to strengthen the panel. In our projects, we use it to reinforce the horizontal axis. In larger stained glass pieces, it can be used in several places for more reinforcement.

Solder

In the world of stained glass, solder is the glue that holds it all together. The solder used in stained glass work has a solid core and is an alloy made of lead, zinc, and tin. Solder is heated until molten with a soldering iron before it's applied to either foil or lead projects. On copper-foiled projects, you'll solder along the entire length of each seam. On leaded projects, you'll apply about a ¼-inch-wide (6 mm) solder seam to each came joint.

Solder is also used to attach the hardware for hanging your finished work. *Tinning* refers to a light coat of solder applied to metal wire, brass shim, or brass lamp caps—just enough to turn the metal silver.

Alloys made from combinations of silver, tin, and copper in various proportions are available as lead-free alternatives, but with varying results. A silver solder is also manufactured to reduce the amount of lead in pieces that will be handled regularly, such as jewelry and boxes. If you're concerned about lead content in your work, you can try these alternatives.

Flux, flux remover

Flux, a chemical agent available in liquid, paste, or gel, plays a crucial role in soldering. It assists in dispersing the heat from the iron, cleans the metal, and allows the solder to flow smoothly and stick to foil and lead.

Flux is applied with a special brush. All types of flux should be removed as soon as possible after the completion of soldering to avoid oxidation on solder or lead. Liquid and gel flux are often water-based so that they clean off easily with water-based flux remover. In most cases, liquid fluxes can also be removed with a bit of liquid detergent and water. To remove paste flux, use a cotton ball moistened with acetone.

I have a preference for the old-fashioned paste flux. I find liquid flux more difficult to work with, since it's easy to spill and evaporates quickly.

SAFETY: If you get flux on your skin, remove it with soap and water immediately, because it will eventually irritate or burn it. Keep your flux brush in a safe place, away from other tools, when you're not using it. Avoid inhaling flux fumes; they are toxic. When you're working with any kind of flux, use good ventilation.

Stained glass cement/glazing compounds

Stained glass cement, a thick, turpentine-based product, glazing compounds, and glass putty are all used for finishing glass panels. However, stained glass cement is your best choice, since its performance surpasses that of old-fashioned glazing compounds and putty. Cement breathes best in the changing temperatures of outdoor weather and also serves to darken leaded came lines, lending panels a finished look.

Cement or glaze must be applied to larger leaded panels that will be exposed to outdoor weather in order to strengthen and weatherproof them. You should also cement or glaze larger indoor projects to give them strength and prevent pieces from shifting or rattling. In either case, always apply the compound to both sides of a panel.

I prefer the black-tinted, premixed cementing compounds. This cement must be turned in the can several

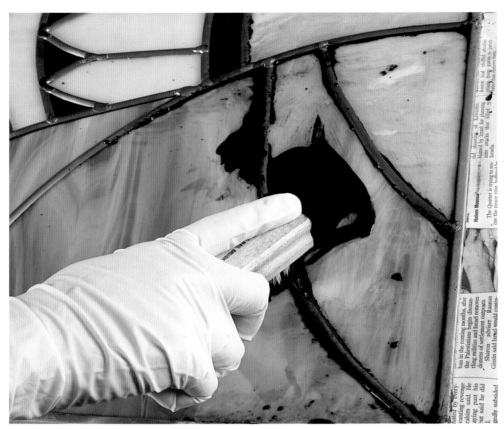

Photo 1

Whiting

Whiting is used to seal the cement or glaze, remove any residue on the glass, and clean the came. Sprinkle a little bit of this powder over the completed panel once the excess compound is removed, then scrub the glass and came with a natural-bristle hand brush (photo 2).

times for a few days to keep it from settling, making the mixing process easier. It has the consistency of a thick mud when stirred.

Before applying cement or glaze, protect your work surface with several layers of paper. Spread the compound on a completed panel with a natural-bristle hand brush, pushing it under each piece of came. Some of it will naturally flow to the back side of the piece (photo 1).

Collect any excess cement or glaze on the brush, and return it to the can. Clean the brush with a nail, between the rows of bristles. After this step, apply powdered whiting (see next section), and brush the entire panel and came with a clean brush.

Turn the panel over (see page 40), and cement the other side using the same process. Clean up the excess cement or glaze compound with whiting, and use another nail to clean out corners and tight points. Soak the cement brush in mineral spirits. Setting time varies with humidity and temperature conditions, but some setting up will occur in a few hours. However, you should allow the project to sit and harden for 24 to 48 hours.

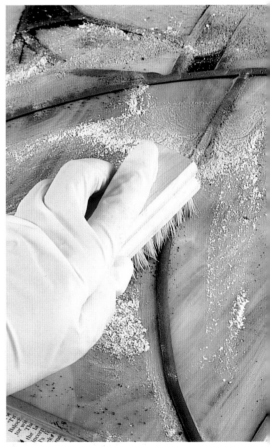

Photo 2

Photo 3

Before using a patina on lines of came, scrub them with a wire brush to remove any oxidation. If solder lines aren't completely clean and fresh or no longer a shiny silver, wipe them lightly with fine steel wool or an abrasive cloth before applying the patina. This might be the case if the project's been sitting around for more than a few days.

Photo 4

To avoid a cloud of dust, use a fine-haired table brush to carefully sweep the whiting into a dustpan (photo 3). Sweep around the table edges as well. Repeat on the other side.

Whiting is also used, in small quantities, to polish stained glass panels. Use an old toothbrush to polish small items. For larger panels of glass, clean them with lint-free paper towels or cotton rags.

Patinas

Patinas are acidic solutions used to change the color of came or solder from silver to (typically) black, copper, or antique brass. This optional step is taken as the very final step after you've finished and cleaned the project.

To apply patinas, follow the manufacturer's instructions carefully. You can shake and pour a small amount of the solution into the cap of the container, or weigh down the bottle so that it doesn't tip over. Use cotton-tipped swabs to brush the patina onto the panel's came and/or solder lines (photos 4 and 5). Change swabs as they get dirty.

Repeat this process until you're satisfied with the results. As the patina dries, use a clean rag or paper towel to skim around each glass edge to remove any excess solution.

SAFETY:
Since patinas are acids, you will probably want to wear gloves when you apply them. You can avoid getting the solution on your hands by using a cotton swab for dipping, but this practice is not guaranteed. Purchase disposable surgical gloves at a medical supply store or pharmacy, or buy a pair of rubber gloves at a hardware store. You should also avoid inhaling patina fumes, so keep your work area well-ventilated.

Photo 5

As you work, not only should you avoid getting the solution on your skin, but you should be careful not to spill it on the glass. If a patina solution dries too long, it may leave an iridized-looking stain. If you goof, stain removers made specifically for stained glass can be used to remedy this problem.

Kraft paper, carbon paper

For making templates and patterns needed to cut glass pieces accurately, use heavyweight kraft paper (available at craft supply stores). A few sheets of carbon paper can be used to trace your enlarged patterns onto this paper.

Waterproof markers

To avoid confusion when working with pattern pieces, use markers and a numbering system to label all the parts of your pattern before you cut them

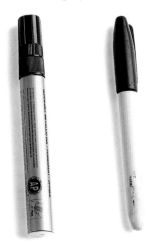

apart. Then, transfer this number to each piece of glass as you cut it. Use a white or gold waterproof marker/pen on dark-colored glass and a black pen on light-colored glass.

These markers also come in handy when you need to mark off an edge that doesn't quite fit the pattern after you've cut the glass. The line will provide you with a guide for grinding away excess glass.

Lint-free cotton rags or paper towels, cotton balls, cotton-tipped swabs

Keep all of these supplies in your workspace for wiping glass clean, applying patinas, lubricating glass cutters, removing flux, polishing projects after they've been brushed with whiting, and general cleaning.

Ammonia-free glass cleaner, rubbing (isopropyl) alcohol

Clean glass cuts more easily than dirty or filmy glass. To clean stained glass, use a glass cleaner that doesn't contain ammonia, since it can interfere with the application of patinas. Instead, use a vinegar-based cleaner or rubbing alcohol.

Tools & Equipment

Many of the tools in the following section are made specifically for stained glass and can be purchased through a stained glass supplier. Once you learn how to make these clever helpers work to your advantage, you'll be able to concentrate on the real joy of being creative with glass.

Pattern shears

Pattern shears are designed specifically to cut out the interior lines of the templates for stained glass panels. As they cut, they leave a thin strip of paper representing the distance between the pieces of glass to be occupied by the heart of the came or the copper foil.

These shears are available in two sizes, one tailored to the needs of copper foil projects (1/32 inch [.75 mm]) and the other made for leaded projects (1/16 inch [1.6 mm]). This slight difference in width can make or break your project when you're working with these two different assembly methods, so make sure to use the right shears for the technique you're using!

When cutting with pattern shears, hold them with the blades perpendicular to the paper and take short strokes, discarding the paper strings as you work.

Display hardware

The most common method of displaying a stained glass panel is to suspend it by one or two lengths of chain attached to a hanger soldered directly into the panel's outer came. For the hanger, you can use a preformed brass hanger, if available, or heavy-gauge wire (often already tinned, or coated with a thin film of solder) that can be twisted into shape before soldering it to the came. If you use regular copper or brass wire, it must be tinned first. You can also cut apart brass-pin backings, and use the center portion, as shown above.

Although many types of chain can be used, I prefer jack chain with links that can be opened and closed with needle-nose pliers. This allows you to attach the chain to hangers, and shorten or lengthen it as needed when hanging the panel.

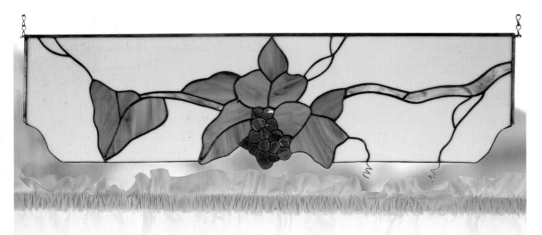

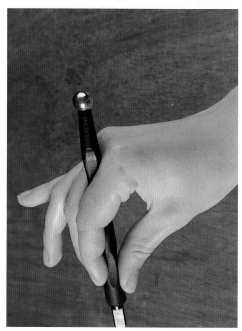

Photo 6

Photo 7

To hold a standard straight cutter, hold it between your first and second finger, with the cutting wheel facing you. Grasp your thumb on the front of the flat hold, and place your first and second fingertips on the back of the thumb rest (photo 6). This will keep the wheel perpendicular to the glass, helping you to maintain control over its movement. Cup your other hand over the cutter with your thumb resting on the top part of the cutter, allowing you to apply downward pressure without straining your wrists (photo 7).

Now, stand with your feet apart. With the line to be scored directly in front of you, pull (don't push!) the cutter along it. Begin at the edge of the glass farthest from you. Use the weight of your shoulders to apply pressure, and avoid twisting your elbows or wrists, even when scoring curves. By using your body and shoulder weight, you can avoid straining your arms and hands. Keep your eye on the front of the cutting wheel to follow the line.

Glass cutters, lubricant

Despite the name, glass cutters don't actually cut glass; rather, they score it by means of a small beveled wheel that rolls across the surface. Almost invisible to the eye, these score lines weaken the glass enough that it can be broken into very specific shapes.

There are lots of styles and shapes of glass cutters. If you're a beginner, a straight, steel-wheel cutter will work well. Other options include comfort grips with long-lasting carbide wheels, self-lubricating cutters, and pistol-grip cutters.

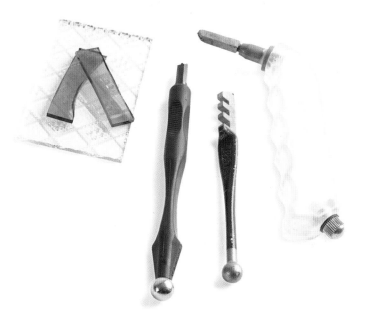

TIPS: Keep the cutting wheel perpendicular to the glass; it must never tilt to the left or right. Scores made with a tilted cutter can break at an angle or fail to break along the whole score. Glass will only break properly if you begin the score on one edge of a piece of glass and continue through to the other. Try to apply even pressure to your cutter as you pull it across the glass, or the score will be uneven in depth, and the glass may not break evenly. Also, keep the speed of your movement even as you pull the cutter along the score line. When you score a line correctly, you should see a barely visible line, not a white, powdery line. If this happens, ease up on the pressure.

Pistol-grip cutters will be more comfortable for you if you have poor wrist or hand strength, but the cutting method is different. To use these cutters, cut away from yourself along a score line, rather than towards you. Consequently, you may find that you have less visibility.

As you're working, you'll need to keep the glass cutter's wheel well-lubricated with oil. Stained glass cutting lubricants are available in oil-based, water-based, and eco-friendly formulas. They all provide ease in cutting and protection for your glass-cutting wheel. For convenience, place several cotton balls in the bottom of an old coffee cup and saturate them with oil. After a few scores, return the cutter to the cup to keep the wheel clean. As the cotton balls get soiled, replace them with new ones. Even if the cup rolls over, the liquid won't spill.

You can learn to cut glass shapes on clear, inexpensive window glass. It's readily available, thin, and cuts easily. Place the cutter at the top edge of the glass and press down vertically—just enough to create a visible scratch on the glass in the direction you wish. Continue smoothly to the other end of the glass sheet. Repeat this process, breaking each score as you go and using multiple cuts to extract the shape you want. With practice, it will begin to feel like a natural process.

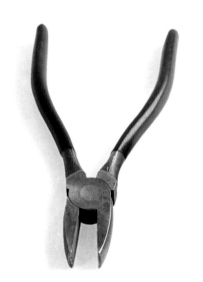

Breaking pliers

Use breaking pliers to remove smaller pieces of glass that you're not able to break comfortably with your hands (see page 31). These smooth-jawed pliers act as an extension of your hand, allowing you to grasp the glass firmly without scratching it.

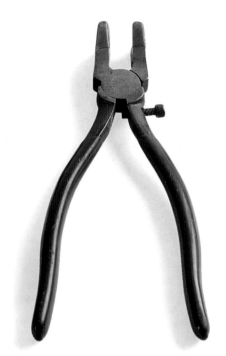

Running pliers

Designed to exert equal amounts of pressure on each side of the score line, running pliers are used to break long scores (whether straight or curved) on large glass pieces. These pliers have two cushioned jaws—one concave and one convex—that serve to exert firm pressure on either side of the score, running the break along its entire length.

Some models have a screw adjustment on the top, allowing you to adjust them according to the glass's thickness. Place the top center of these adjustable pliers over the end of the score line, tighten the screw on top lightly, and release the screw back three-quarters of a turn. Then squeeze them until the glass breaks.

SAFETY: Always wear safety glasses when cutting or breaking glass. Should a splinter of glass get in your eye, don't rub it! Instead, rinse it away with clean running water over your open eye. If thorough rinsing doesn't work, see a doctor right away.

Grozing pliers

Grozing pliers have grooved jaws with little teeth that can nibble and chip away excess glass, allowing you to smooth sharp edges and round corners. They're particularly helpful for trimming away more glass than a grinder is designed to remove (see next section). You should always use them over a trashcan or some other container, since glass chips tend to fly and scatter during this process.

Glass grinder, face shield

A glass grinder is used to grind the edges of glass until they're smoothly sanded and perpendicular. Equipped with interchangeable bits, this electric-powered tool allows you to create more intricate shapes and curves than with a glass cutter and grozing pliers. An array of grinding bits are available with varying circumferences.

This piece of equipment has a water reservoir and a rotating, diamond-coated head. Soft water is recommended. To provide longer life to your grinder, add coolant to the water reservoir, which decreases friction and prevents the diamond bits from rubbing off. To extend its life, move the height of the bit as it wears down.

SAFETY: While you should always wear safety glasses when you cut and break glass, you need the added protection of a face shield when grinding glass. Most grinders come with a plastic one, or you can purchase one separately. A helpful accessory that may or may not be included with your grinder is a pair of plastic "thumb savers" or "glass grippers" that are made to protect your fingers when grinding very small pieces.

Grinding the edges of glass is imperative for copper foiling. The degree of perfection can be less for leaded work, but it's still important to even up the glass edges for insertion into the came.

To use a grinder, place the cut glass flat on the grinder's work surface, and push the edge of it gently but firmly against the spinning bit (photo 8).

Photo 8

21

The water should wash away any glass dust, so if you see dry dust on the grinding bit, add more water to the reservoir. Avoid overfilling it to prevent the water from spraying on you.

To check your progress, dry the glass piece thoroughly, then compare it to its pattern (photo 9). If glass shows around the pattern, continue grinding those areas until the piece matches perfectly. (You can use a marker to draw lines, if needed.) The smaller-diameter grinding bits allow you to grind out tiny grooves and small areas.

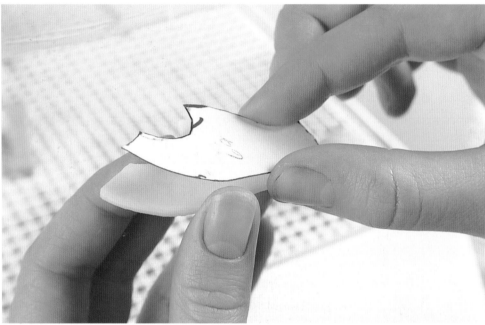

Photo 9

Grinding stone

A simple alternative to a grinder is a grinding stone. After wetting it, you simply file down the glass edges by rubbing the stone against it. This can be a very laborious process, however, and may leave you running to the nearest supplier to buy a grinder instead!

Lead vise

Before lead came can be used in a project, it must be stretched, both to straighten it and increase its strength. For this purpose, you can use a small, grooved vise that is spring-loaded. The vise mounts to your workbench or table with a nail or screw.

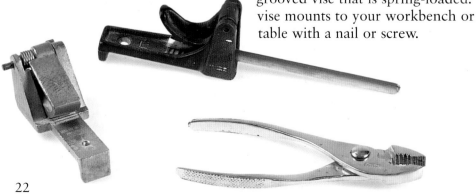

To stretch the came, begin by cutting a manageable length for your workbench. Insert one end of it into the vise's jaws with the channel facing up. Give the top of the vise a firm tap with a hammer or pliers to make sure its teeth get a good grip on the lead. Untwist the came so that it's straight, then grip the other free end with slip-joint pliers, standing at the opposite end of your workbench.

Hold the pliers in front of you, bracing yourself against the table, since lead can snap or pull from your grasp (photo 10). You can place a folded towel beneath the pliers in case the lead pulls out, saving your knuckles from smacking the tabletop if the came happens to break. Larger came sizes typically don't stretch as far, or break as easily, as smaller sizes do.

Pull firmly with the strength of your arms until the lead is straight and taut, so that it adds about 1 to 3 inches (2.5 to 7.6 cm), to the length of the came, depending on the size of the lead.

Photo 10

Hacksaw, electric cutting saw

Brass, zinc, and copper are all much harder than lead, so you can't cut them with nippers. To cut an occasional piece of came made from any of these metals, you can use a hand-held hacksaw with a fine-toothed blade.

After marking the angle you need to cut on the top face of the came, hold it in place with your hand and begin sawing on the mark until the blade catches on the metal. Continue sawing from the front to back until you complete the cut.

If you intend to do a lot of work with brass, zinc, or copper came, you'll probably want to go ahead and purchase a more efficient alternative—a small electric, metal-cutting saw.

Lead nippers (dykes)

You'll need a pair of lead nippers to cut lead came. These special pliers have a flat jaw and an angled one, resulting in a flush (or straight) cut on the portion of the came toward which the flat jaw is aimed, and a V-shaped cut on the other piece (photos 11 to 13). You can use leftover V-shaped pieces for bumpers to temporarily hold glass pieces in place as you measure and fit your permanent pieces of came.

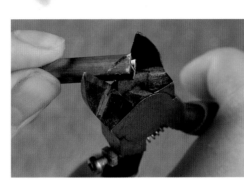

Photo 11

Photo 12

Photo 13

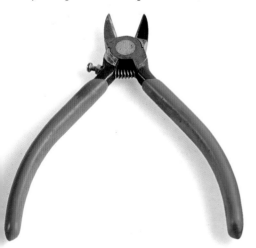

Metal files

These files, which come in a variety of styles, are used to smooth the corner edges of came after you assemble a piece.

Crimper or burnisher

When you're assembling with copper foil, it's applied and folded over the edges of each cut piece of glass. Then it has to be flattened, burnished, and crimped around the glass edges to remove air bubbles and ensure a tight, even seal.

To make this job as simple as possible, you'll need a commercial crimper, a tool that will perform all these jobs in one step. There are many styles available from which to choose.

23

However, you can also use a wood fid, dowel, chopstick, or any found tool that works for you to rub or burnish the foil. When you're using highly irregular-shaped pieces, such as geodes and nuggets, you'll use this simpler tool because of the uneven textures.

Horseshoe nails

Pounded directly into the wooden top of your work surface with a hammer, horseshoe nails are used to hold came and glass pieces in place as you assemble your project.

These nails are sold by weight, and a #5 nail (50 mm) works well for most jobs. Make sure the nails are placed so that their flat sides abut the came or bumpers. Remove them by rocking them side to side, taking care not to bend their tips. With proper care, you should be able to use the same ones for many years.

Glazing hammer

You can use a small household hammer for pounding horseshoe nails, but a glazing hammer is more versatile. This tool has a dual-faced head; one side is plastic, the other rubber. The plastic side works well for hammering horseshoe nails, and the rubber side can be used to tap wide-edged glass into lengths of came.

Photo 14

Wire brushes

To clean lead came prior to fluxing and soldering, you'll need to scrub each joint with a wire brush (photo 14). Prior to applying patina, use the brush to scrub the entire length of came before wiping it off with a clean rag or paper towel.

Flux Brushes

To apply flux, you'll also use a special brush (see picture on page 14). Because flux is corrosive, you should store your flux brushes away from other tools. A jar works well for this purpose.

Natural-bristle hand brushes

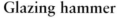

These small brushes have traditionally been made for scrubbing hands and nails, but now they're a staple item for stained glass. This wooden brush with straight bristles is used for cementing and applying whiting after cementing.

Soldering iron and holder

This type of soldering iron, made specifically for stained glass work, has a heat-resistant handle fitted with replaceable chisel-shaped tips. For the projects in this book, you'll need an iron that heats to a temperature of 900 to 1,000°F (482 to 538°C), and a ¼-inch (6 mm) tip to accompany it. Typically, these irons are either lightweight and slim, made to be held like a pencil, or slightly heavier, made to be held with an overhand grip. Purchase this piece of equipment from a glass studio or supplier.

Keep a damp, chemical-free sponge available to periodically clean off the tip while you're soldering. Doing this eliminates contaminant from the solder line, which is especially important when you're using copper foil.

Table Brush

This standard brush has soft bristles, perfect for catching the smallest bit of glass and removing them from harm's way. Don't ever use your bare hands to try to whisk away glass particles. Use this brush after each work session.

Light box/table

A light box or table may give you more workspace while allowing you to see pieces of glass lighted as they'll appear once they're displayed. The box also can be used for lighting and tracing patterns, and for cutting glass by the English method (see page 29).

You can purchase a light box, or you can make one by using ¼-inch-thick (6 mm) frosted glass inlaid in a wooden frame/box with a florescent light mounted inside. If you wish, you can add legs to the box to make it freestanding.

Workspace & Safety

Stained glass is a rewarding hobby, but not one that's without risks. You'll be working with sharp glass pieces, high temperatures, lead, and various chemicals. Protect yourself, your family, and your pets by following the safety tips mentioned throughout this book. Please read these guidelines carefully, and keep them in mind as you set up your workspace.

Even though it's an enviable luxury, a separate studio is not necessary to begin working with stained glass. You simply need an area with good lighting and ventilation, at least one electrical outlet with a grounded circuit, and easy access to running water. Choose a location that isn't close to your kitchen or any other area where food is prepared. Never allow children or animals to enter your workspace unless you'll be able to keep your eyes on them at all times.

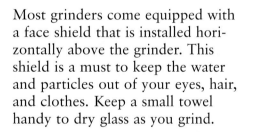

You'll also need a steady, level table or workbench with a surface that's above your standing waist height. You can use an existing table or have one made to suit your needs, which is really the ideal thing to do. Choose a height that's comfortable for you to prevent back strain when working. Since you'll be standing to do most glass cutting, give your feet some comfort and relief by placing a sturdy, non-slip floor mat cushion beside your workbench.

In addition to a number of other tasks, you'll use this table for cutting and assembling stained glass panels, which means it's going to get hammered full of nail holes and burned by soldering. For this reason, any tabletop surface that you use should be at least ⅝-inch (1.6 cm) thick. You can replace this top as it gets too full of holes with years of use.

Keep your workspace clean, well organized, and free of clutter. If you have a glass grinder, place it on a tray in one corner. Protect the surrounding area from spraying water and glass dust by using a plastic-covered backsplash around the sides and back of the grinder or a backshield made for the grinder.

Most grinders come equipped with a face shield that is installed horizontally above the grinder. This shield is a must to keep the water and particles out of your eyes, hair, and clothes. Keep a small towel handy to dry glass as you grind.

Wear safety glasses when you're scoring and breaking glass. Use a fine, soft table brush and dustpan to sweep off your workbench as you cut and assemble.

In addition, store your tools together after each session, away from flux and chemicals and within easy reach of your workbench. Sheets of glass should be stored vertically and can be sorted by size and color. Never lift them above your head!

When working with lead came, wash your hands frequently between steps and use disposable towels to dry them. Wear gloves when working with acid patinas.

When you're fluxing or soldering, run a small fan to draw away any fumes, especially if you don't have good ventilation in your work area.

In general, use common sense about caring for your workspace as well as your health. Always read the labels of any products that you use. Proceed slowly as you learn how to best utilize tools and supplies.

Techniques

At first glance, stained glass might seem as if it's a very complex art. After all, given the gorgeous end results, you might think that it can't be easy.

Although some of the specific techniques might take some time to master, none of them are inherently difficult. With practice, you'll be able to master this art, and the learning process can be very exciting.

This chapter describes, in sequence, various techniques you'll use to create stained glass projects. The sections that follow show, among other things, how to work with a pattern and cut glass. You'll also learn the secrets of assembling glass with both copper foil and came. How-to photos and steps will guide you smoothly through the process.

If you're just beginning, take time to read all the way through this chapter before beginning one of the projects. You'll save a lot of frustration if you familiarize yourself with the techniques first. As you work on various projects, thumb back to sections as needed for reference.

Making & Using Patterns

All stained glass pieces begin with a full-sized template, similar to a large map. Each project in this book is accompanied by a small black-and-white template that you can enlarge to the finished size indicated or vary to accommodate your specific needs. Without it, you won't be able to precisely fit together all the pieces of your glass puzzle.

If you're using the first method described below, you'll make a traced and numbered pattern on heavyweight kraft paper from the original template. The second method, called the English method, allows you to work directly from the pattern, and only works with clear and light-colored glass.

Working with a Cut-Apart Pattern

The most popular and accurate way of cutting out the interlocking pieces of a stained glass panel is to trace the pattern onto heavyweight kraft paper before cutting it into individual pieces. Use the directions that follow to guide you.

1. Begin by making an enlarged copy of the pattern with a photo-copy machine or enlarger (small overhead projector). To transfer the template, spread out sturdy kraft paper on your work surface. Place a sheet or two of carbon paper face-down on top of it before placing the full-size template over the carbon paper. To keep them in place as you work, tack down all three layers to the work surface with horse-shoe nails.

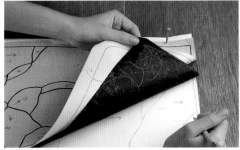

Photo 1

2. Use a pencil or pen to firmly trace over all the pattern lines. Assign a number to each piece of the design. If you're using glass with a pattern or grain, draw arrows indicating the direction you need in the project. For instance, if your piece includes sky and backgrounds, you may want the grain to be horizontal, contributing to the effect of the design.

3. Take out a few nails so that you can lift up one end of the pattern and carbon paper to make sure you traced all the pattern lines, num-

Photo 2

Photo 3

bers, and arrows (photo 1). Then remove the rest of the nails, and lay the original template aside.

4. With regular scissors, cut around the outer edge of the enlarged pattern. Then, cut out the individual pieces using the appropriate pattern shears. For copper-foiled projects, you'll need $^1/_{32}$-inch (.75 mm) shears. For leaded projects, you'll need $^1/_{16}$-inch (1.6 mm) shears.

5. Center the shears directly over the pattern line, perpendicular to the paper. Cut in short strokes, primarily at the top of the blades, discarding the paper strips as you go (photo 2).

6. Use the pattern pieces you've cut to trace the designs on the appropriate pieces of glass, leaving enough space around each piece to cut and break them out comfortably, at least $^1/_4$ to $^1/_2$ inch (.6 to 1.3 cm). If you'll be cutting more than one piece from one sheet of glass, minimize waste by spending some time arranging your pattern pieces economically to fit the sheet, but leave at least one inch (2.5 cm) of space around each. To trace, use a black permanent marker on lighter-colored glass, and a white or gold marker on darker glass (photo 3). Don't forget to copy the number from each pattern piece to its matching shape on the glass.

Using the English Method of Cutting

This method is a less laborious way to cut out a design. The full-sized template is used as your guide for cutting, skipping the use of individual, puzzle-like pattern pieces. This method works well *only* if you're using very transparent or light-colored glass. Several of the projects included in this book require clear textured glass and bevels, and these types of glass work well with this method.

If your project includes even a couple of opaque pieces, you can't use this method. Instead, use the former method of cutting all the pattern pieces apart. The following steps describe the specifics of this method.

1. Instead of making a pattern and tracing each individual pattern piece onto each piece of glass to be used, place each sheet on top of the full-size pattern where it belongs. The pattern line beneath the glass serves as your guide for scoring, just as the traced marks on the glass did in the first method we introduced. For better visibility, work on a light table or over white paper (photo 4).

2. Turn the piece of glass and template as needed to position the score

Photo 6

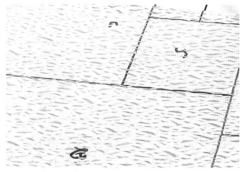
Photo 4

Photo 5

line in front of you (photo 5). Score on the middle to the inside of the pattern line to allow room for foil or came. Number the pieces as you go.

3. Score and break pieces as described in the next section.

4. When they're all laid out on the full-size template, your glass pieces should still have a bit of space between each piece to accommodate foil or lead.

Scoring & Breaking the Glass

Even though it's referred to as "cutting the glass," you'll really be scoring and breaking it into specific shapes. This process often takes more than one or two cuts; for instance, you can't cut out circular pieces all at once. Instead, you'll make a series of scores and breaks, gradually "carving" away excess glass to reveal the desired shape (photo 6).

Before you begin, review the description of how to hold and use a glass cutter on page 19, and remember to practice your cutting technique on plain window glass before risking more expensive stained glass.

One note before you get started: Don't be discouraged if glass breaks

the wrong way, or if you cut a piece too small, too large, or just plain wrong. It happens to the most experienced artists! Chalk it up to the learning process, and move on. However, if you find yourself making the same mistake on a shape after a couple of tries, try doing the cutting sequence in a different order (see the troubleshooting section on page 126). If you get frustrated with anything come back to it at another time.

The following steps will guide you in this process of scoring and breaking glass.

1. If you're cutting several pieces from a single sheet of glass, your first step will be to cut the sheet apart into more manageable pieces (photos 7 and 8). Begin by placing the wheel of your cutter near the top edge of the glass. Press down vertically, pulling in the direction you wish, using just enough pressure to make a visible scratch. When you're cutting along a line, score along the middle to the inside of the line to allow room for the copper foil or came.

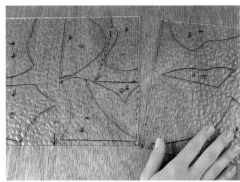

Photo 7

Photo 8

Photo 9

the middle of a score or making more than a subtle change in direction. Never go back over a score line once it's been made, since this might ruin the sharp edge of the cutting wheel. Remember to keep the wheel of your cutter clean and lubricated with oil.

3. As you make each score, break the glass along the score line while the surface tension is fresh. (A line made 24 hours prior seldom breaks correctly!) When working with a piece of glass that's comfortable to hold in your hands, use your thumbs and knuckles to make the break. To do this, grip the glass with a hand on either side of the score with your thumbs close to the bottom of it on the upper face. In

Photo 10

addition, bend the first knuckle of each hand directly underneath the glass (photo 10). Apply equal pressure from both hands, while pulling the glass down and apart. If the piece doesn't break easily, you can try using your pliers for more leverage (see step 4).

Photo 11

4. If you're working with a piece of glass that has a side too small to break comfortably with your hands, you can use breaking pliers. Grip the glass near the bottom of the score on the small edge with the ends of the jaws of the pliers parallel to the score (photo 11).

Photo 12

Photo 13

Grasping the glass on the opposite side of the score (photo 11) with your other hand, gently pull the pliers downward and apart to break the glass. For very small pieces, you can use two pairs of pliers, as shown in photos 12 and 13.

Photo 14

2. As you pull the cutter, maintain its vertical position to ensure a nice, perpendicular edge on your glass. Whether you're cutting a straight or a curved line, you should score glass from one edge of the sheet to another, using a single, smooth, continuous motion (photo 9). Avoid lifting the cutter from the glass in

31

5. To break out a long score on a larger piece of glass, use running pliers. Grasp the edge of the glass in the full width of the pliers' jaws, centering them over the score line about ½-inch (1.3 cm) from the edge (photo 14, page 31). (Many models of these pliers have a line scribed on the outside of the upper, concave jaw that can be used to accurately align them with the score line.) Squeeze the handles gently to run the break up the score line.

6. After you've cut the sheet into smaller, more manageable pieces, you can begin to score and trim away the excess glass from around each pattern shape.

Grozing & Grinding

Even if you've scored and broken your glass with expert care and precision, the edges of your pieces will probably still have uneven areas that don't quite match your pattern. But, fortunately, there's a simple solution. You can groze and grind the edges until they match, as described below.

1. To check the cutting job on each piece, match the cut glass piece up with its pattern piece by number. Then hold the two up to compare them (photo 15). If edges of glass extend beyond the pattern piece, hold the glass with the pattern on top of it over a trashcan or other container. Then nibble away the areas with your grozing pliers until the outline matches the pattern (photo 16).

2. If you're preparing pieces for a copper-foiled project, you'll need to use your grinder after grozing to make the edges as smooth and exact as possible. Be careful not to grind away too much glass during this process, so take things slowly. If you've never used a glass grinder before, take the time to read the manufacturer's operating and care instructions carefully. For leaded projects, you can skip the grinding process unless the glass doesn't fit correctly into the came during assembly (see pages 36 to 39). Dry each piece thoroughly after grinding.

Photo 15

Photo 16

TIPS:

• When cutting a piece with a sharp point, cut away from the point, and make the break at the larger end. Doing this gives you room to hold on with your pliers, and decreases your chances of breaking off the slimmer, sharper point.

• When scoring and breaking curves, always break the convex (inside) curves first to save glass. This way, if you break off too much of a curve, you can retrace the pattern piece as needed and try again. Score and break the concave (outside) curves next.

• To handle very deep or long curves, you might need to make several, progressively larger scallop-shaped scores to deepen the curve to the pattern line.

• Score and break the straight lines last, they're the easiest.

Methods of Assembly for Glass Pieces

The stained glass projects in this book are assembled with channeled came, copper foil, or a combination of the two methods. Leading is the traditional way of assembling panels, lending strength to combined glass pieces. Copper foil involves more soldering, and works well for assembling more intricate panels.

Copper Foil Assembly

If you want to attach pieces of glass together without using channeled came, you can use the copper foil method of assembly. This technique was first adapted during the late 1800s to make Art Nouveau lamp shades and other pieces. Since lead wasn't pliable enough to be shaped into the curvy, intricate shapes of the patterns, flexible copper or brass channeling was used instead as a base for soldering.

This method results in finer line quality than lead does, and works well for smaller, more detailed pieces. With copper foiling, you don't have the advantage of being able to hide imperfect edges under came, but some beginners find this to be an easier method to learn. The following steps will tell you how to apply copper foil.

1. After you've finished cutting all of your glass pieces, assemble them on top of the full-size template with which you began your project. Place them in their proper spots as if you're piecing together a puzzle. If your pieces matched their patterns exactly after grinding and grozing, they should fit perfectly, with just a slight bit of space between each shape. If they don't fit exactly here and there, use the individual patterns and spend a little more time grinding them to fit where they don't.

2. Choose a width of copper foil that will adequately cover the edge of the glass you're using, with room to fold it slightly over both faces of the piece. Thick or heavily textured glass, for instance, will require wider foil than thin or non-textured glass. If you plan to apply a patina to the finished panel, remember to use foil with a backing that will match.

3. Choose a piece to begin copper foiling. Peel away the paper backing from the foil, and center the adhesive side of it along the edge of the glass. For pieces that don't form part of the outside edges of the finished panel (interior pieces), you can start and end (overlap) foiling at any point. You'll eventually foil the exterior edges of your piece, or use a came border. If you're making a panel that you plan to frame with came, you won't need to foil the exterior edges.

4. Center the adhesive side of the foil on the edge of the glass piece, and begin pressing the strip into place. Make sure that it's even and centered as you work your way around the glass. At this point in the process, it's easy to peel back some of the foil and readjust it before folding it down over the edges (photo 17). End by overlap-

Photo 17

ping the foil by about ¼ inch (6 mm) over the starting point.

Note: There are now gadgets on the market that are made specifically to help you center foil, if you find this process too tedious.

Photo 18

5. Press down the outer edges of the foil over the front and back faces of the glass, folding the corners down neatly with your fingers. (Now you'll see why it was so important to center the foil along the edges!) While doing this, resist sliding your fingers along the sides of the foil, or you may get a nasty cut. Use a crimper or burnisher to seal the edges, smoothing out any air bubbles and forming a tight seal (photo 18).

6. Inspect your foiled piece to make sure you've applied the foil evenly. You can use a razor-blade cutter to trim away any obvious areas that are too lopsided, or peel the foil off and start again if the visual problem can't be fixed with a slight trimming. With some practice, applying the foil evenly can become second nature.

Soldering of Copper Foil Panels

If you've foiled and trimmed your glass pieces carefully, the assembly of your copper foil panel should go smoothly. The following steps will tell you how to do this.

Photo 19

TACK-SOLDERING

Once you position the pieces of your panel, you'll need to tack them together at a few joints with bits of solder to hold them in place before you begin doing the real work of creating solder beads. The following section will warm you up for the job ahead.

1. Assemble all the foiled pieces on your work surface on top of the full-size template, using the numbers as a guide. The pieces should butt up lightly against each other (photo 19). Don't worry if you notice some small spaces between edges because the solder will fill these.

2. Pay attention to the exterior lines of the pattern, using them to line up the outer edges of the piece. They must be straight.

3. Once the borders of the panel are even and square, you'll tack-solder a few joints together to hold them in place.

4. Turn on your soldering iron, and allow it to heat up for a minute or two. Meanwhile, apply a bit of flux at several seams where the glass joins along the outside edges of the panel.

5. Unwind about 6 to 8 inches (15.2 to 20.3 cm) of 50/50 solder from the spool. Hold the spool in one hand, and position the end of the solder just above one of the freshly fluxed joints.

6. Holding your soldering iron in your other hand, touch the hot tip of the iron to the top of the solder wire, and press the molten solder down onto the foil seam, just long enough for the solder to adhere to the foil. It shouldn't take more than a second or two. Repeat this process to tack down more outer edge joints until the panel is stable around the edges.

7. Flux and tack-solder some of the interior seams together on the panel until the seams feel as though they're tightly held in place.

FLAT-FILLING

The subsequent part of soldering in the copper foil method is called flat-filling. This means that you'll run just enough solder into the seams between glass pieces to fill them. Read through this section carefully before you begin.

Photo 20

1. When you're ready, begin by applying flux to the seam you plan to flat-fill first. You can do the seams in any order. Hold the tip of the solder wire over the seam, and heat a bit of it until melted, then drop it onto the seam and drag it along an inch (2.5 cm) or so.

2. Keep moving the iron along the seam, adding solder as you go. Continue melting solder in this fashion, pulling it along the seam to fill in the spaces between the pieces and make the copper foil turn silver (photo 20).

3. If you plan to use came around the border, begin flat-filling about ¼ inch (6 mm) from the panel's outer edges; otherwise the soldered edge won't fit into the came's channel.

HIGH-BEADING THE SEAMS

Once the seams are flat-filled, you'll go back over the seams to make them attractively finished. To do this, you'll smooth out the solder line and run a high bead of 60/40 solder on top of them—a slightly raised, rounded line of solder. Due to a higher tin content, the 60/40 solder cools more slowly than the 50/50 version, so you'll be able to manipulate it more effectively into a smooth finish.

1. As in the process of flat-filling, you'll begin to make a bead by holding the iron's hot tip against the end of the solder wire. This time, however, touch the *top side* of the iron with the solder wire, and allow gravity to pull the molten solder to the underside of the tip so that it forms a bubble.

2. Drag the bubble along the seam, adding more solder as needed.

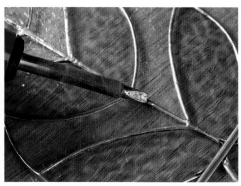
Photo 21

When you're working with molten solder, you'll notice that it flows and levels out to form a smooth bead. This can take some practice, so be prepared to learn your timing on this maneuver (photo 21).

3. To smoothly join lines of solder at a joint where they meet, move up the joint just enough to re-melt the adjoining line of solder, then smooth out the seam as much as possible. You can smooth out any bumps in the solder by holding the iron in the same position that you've been using and gently moving it up and down.

4. As soon as you've finished soldering one side of a panel, clean the flux off of the seams. If you used paste flux, wipe the seams with a cotton ball moistened with acetone. To clean liquid or gel flux, use a commercial flux remover, following the manufacturer's instructions. The panel doesn't have to be perfectly clean yet, but you should take the time to remove the flux.

5. Carefully turn the panel over (see page 40), and finish the seams with a high bead as you did on the reverse.

6. Add outer came as required using bumpers of the same size and insert hangers where required. Attach outer came to any outer foil seams that extend to the panel's edge with tack-soldering. Remove all flux residue (photo 23). (Flip ahead to page 38 for instructions on how to do these final things.)

Photo 23

SPECIAL-EFFECT SOLDERING:

• Intentional large holes between pieces of glass, created for the purposes of your design, may be filled in with scraps of lead and soldered over (photo 24). Textures in these areas can be created by lightly dragging the iron and lifting it up, purposely leaving a rough surface (photo 25). Fill in the spaces slowly, allowing the solder to solidify. Then add a little flux to put a high smooth finish on the area.
• To add solder details, such as dots or "eyes," use 60/40 solder. On a finished, clean panel drop a spot of solder onto the seamline to create the appearance of a raised eye (photo 26).

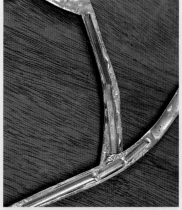
Photo 24

Photo 25

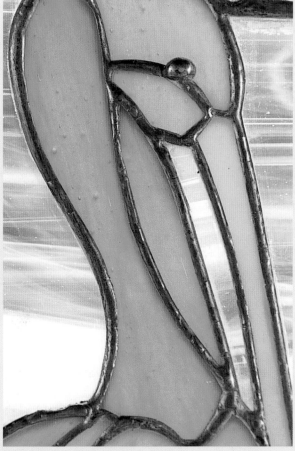
Photo 26

Assembling Leaded Panels with Came

The traditional method of assembling glass panels uses a metal framework composed of came pieces soldered at each joint. Leaded panels can be assembled with lead, zinc, brass, and/or copper came. The came not only holds the glass together, but defines the lines in the panel's design. The edge of each glass piece abuts the heart of the came, which is surrounded by the leaves (figure 1). In most instances, the heart is approximately $\frac{1}{16}$-inch (1.5 mm) thick, no matter how wide the came. For this reason, the pattern lines in leaded glass patterns are assumed to be this size.

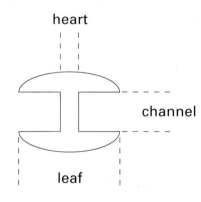

Figure 1

If you've done your homework, and cut all the pieces according to your pattern, you won't have much trouble fitting the pieces together like a jigsaw puzzle. But, if some of them don't fit exactly, you may be able to fix the problem with a bit of shaping (see page 32 on grozing and grinding). Keep in mind that the glass edges will be hidden underneath the came, and they don't have to be shaped as they do for copper foiling.

Depending on the panel design, it may make sense to begin assembling in a corner, on an edge, or even in the middle of the pattern. For this reason, each leaded project in this book has numbered pieces indicating a logical sequence for assembling them.

In most of the projects in this book, lead is used for the interior pieces, while the outside is assembled with lighter-weight zinc came. Zinc is a good choice for square or rectangular panels because it provides excellent support without unnecessary weight.

The following illustrated steps take you through the process of assembling a particular panel. In this case, notice that we begin assembling at the top of the piece. Although the order of assembly varies in the projects, these steps will show you how to use bumpers, cut the lead, and shape it as needed.

1. Brush off your work surface before you begin, then place the template flat on your table, positioning it so that you're starting at the point closest to you. (In this case, we're assembling with the template positioned upside down—in other words, from the panel's top across to the bottom. This position makes it easier to negotiate the curves.)

2. Place the matching glass pieces on the template, using the numbers as a guide (photo 27). There will be a bit of space between the pieces.

3. You'll need horseshoe nails and bumpers (scrap lead pieces the same size as the final came) to hold each piece in place while you're adding it to the panel. Keep in mind that you're building the panel one piece at a time. In this case, we're starting

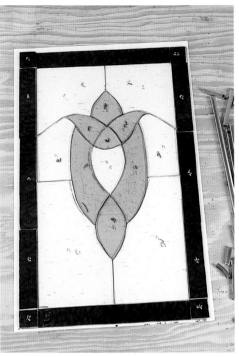

Photo 27

at one end of the panel with a glass piece that will be held in place on one side by the frame. To secure your first piece of glass, use a hacksaw to cut a scrap of border zinc to fit along the outside edge.

Photo 28

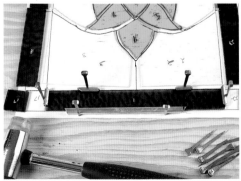

Photo 29

(You must cut zinc with a saw, in contrast to lead that is stretched and then cut with lead nippers.) Use several lead came scraps to shore up the rest of the glass edges. Hammer horseshoe nails with their flat edges against the came to hold the pieces in place (photos 28 and 29).

4. Now you'll cut the first piece of interior lead came that will become a part of the final panel. Cut a foot (30.5 cm) or more of lead with a flat cut on the left end. Position this cut end along the left edge of the glass and across the whole length, on top of the bumpers. Use a nail to mark the other end (photo 30), and cut it flat with your nippers. Replace the bumpers with this length of lead.

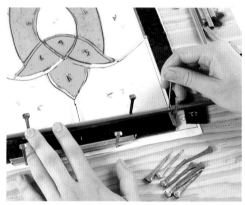
Photo 30

5. Continue by adding another piece of glass next to the first, following the numbered sequence. Remove nails as needed in order to slide in adjacent glass pieces, using

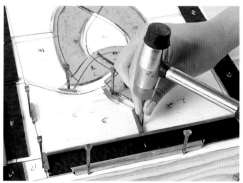
Photo 31

bumpers to hold each new piece in place (photo 31). (Notice that we're working upwards and filling the center of the design. The vertical border lines lend strength to the panel, so always use an unbroken length of came for long lines such as these.)

6. When you lead curved pieces, you'll need to mark and cut the came at angles where the lines meet (photo 32). Since gaps will be covered with solder later, cut the came so that it fits comfortably. Don't force it into place, or it will throw things out of alignment.

Photo 32

7. After the central piece is fitted into the Y-shaped joint, you'll cut the longest curved line next. To do this, bend a length of came slightly longer than the line, using the bumpers as a guide (photo 33). This extra length gives you room for error.

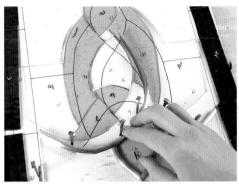
Photo 33

8. As you continue adding glass pieces, wrap the edges of came smoothly around them, cutting pieces as needed with the flat side of the nippers. Then, fit them together snugly (photo 34). (Never try to bend lead around corners or sharp points. Use two pieces of lead instead.)

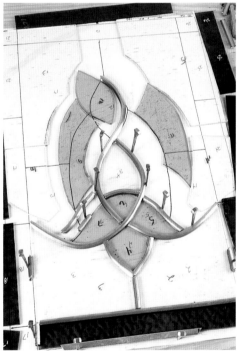
Photo 34

9. Continue to build your panel by adding more pieces and nailing them in place (photo 35). Once the inner part of the panel is fitted and nailed, you'll be ready to add the glass border pieces. As a part of this process, measure and cut a long length of came to fit along the left side (photo 36).

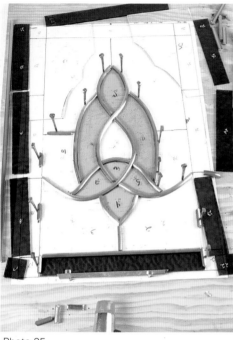

Photo 35

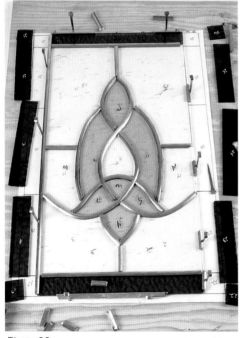

Photo 36

10. Add more pieces until the glass border is in place and the outside edges are all secured with zinc bumpers in preparation for adding the zinc frame (photo 37).

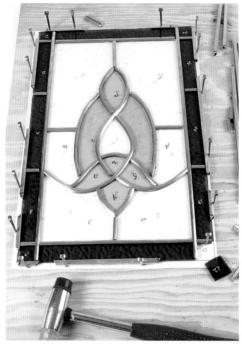

Photo 37

11. To add the frame, position the first piece of came along the right side, on top of the bumpers. Use a saw to miter the edge where it meets the corner of the panel. Then, position the second piece that goes along the bottom edge, and mark the next angle to cut (photo 38).

Photo 38

Note: When all the pieces are nailed down, the lead lines should be straight and any curves should be smooth and flowing. Keep in mind that the solder joints will hide the cuts.

12. When everything is in place, and nails are fitted around the edges, you can add the hangers to the frame. To do this, remove the nails from one side of the outer edge, lift up the piece of came, and insert a tinned hanger into the came channel (see page 41). Reposition the came with the hanger out. Repeat this process on the other side.

13. Before soldering, use the wire brush to clean each came joint, and then flux the joints before soldering them. Strive to make a smooth, clean, overlapping joint, as shown (photos 39 and 40).

14. When all the joints are soldered, clean off the flux, carefully turn the panel over (see page 40). Repeat the soldering process on the back side.

15. Do a final check of your finished panel to make sure that you didn't miss any joints that need soldering. Clean the piece, and add chain to the hangers.

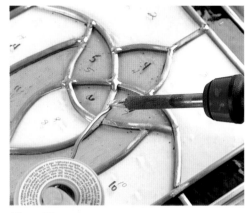

Photo 39

Photo 40

Assembling Panels that Combine Lead and Copper Foil

In stained glass, you have the option of combining copper foil and lead in one panel. These projects can be challenging to assemble, but the results are beautiful.

If a project contains a group of copper-foiled pieces that touch one another, grind, foil, and solder these pieces together as if they're a separate unit, leaving the edges exposed (no foil) where they'll be leaded. After this, high-bead both sides of the copper-foiled unit up to the edges, allowing room for the lead to overlap.

If you're placing foiled pieces whose edges pass *underneath* lead lines, insert the edges into each came channel on either side. Such pieces are soldered later as a part of the final construction (photo 41). When a small foiled piece cuts *through* a lead line (photo 42), cut the lead pieces on either side of it before dropping in the piece.

After all the pieces are in place, wire-brush the lead joints and spots where the foiled pieces meet the lead. Flux these areas and solder them, using a very small amount of solder for the foiled joints. After the front is soldered, turn the panel over and solder the exposed copper-foil seams.

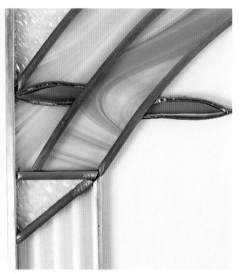

Photo 41

Photo 42

Overlays

An overlay is a piece added to the front of the panel once it is finished. An overlay can be composed of a foiled, tinned, and cleaned piece of glass, shaped pieces of wire, or shapes cut from sheets of metal. The overlay is tack-soldered onto the piece as a final step.

To add an overlay, position it on the panel, and apply a small amount of flux on either side of the piece where it joins the lead or foil line. Tack-solder the piece in place. Don't allow the flux or solder to seep underneath the overlay.

When using a patina, it's recommended that you apply it to the overlay before attaching it, then reapply it to any solder joints (photos 43 and 44).

Photo 45

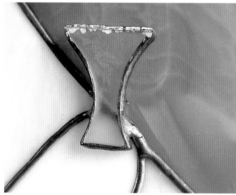

Photo 43

Photo 44

Turning Over Panels During Construction

Until it has been soldered on both sides, a stained glass panel is a somewhat fragile thing. After soldering the first side, you'll need to carefully turn the panel over, in its fragile state, to solder the other side. Use the following technique to avoid damaging your panel.

To do this properly, slide about half of the panel over the edge of your work table, toward yourself, supporting the bottom edge with one hand.

Photo 46

With the other hand, grasp the edge of the panel's top edge and allow it to drop into an upright position in your lower hand, balancing the center on the table's edge (photo 45). Lift up the panel so that its lower edge is positioned toward the back of the workbench, leaving a space behind it that is at least half the panel's width. Move your hands around to the sides to grasp them at the panel's top. In a quick, even motion, allow the panel to descend to the table with gravity guiding you (photo 46). Slide the panel backward onto the worktable. Now you're ready to work on the backside of the panel. Once soldered, the panel will have much more strength, making it easier to clean and handle.

Attachments for Hanging Panels

A popular and attractive way of hanging stained glass panels is inserting pre-made brass hangers into the tops of the two side pieces of the came frame. You'll do this once you've assembled your panel, and all pieces, including the frame, are nailed into place (to make sure that everything fits).

To add these hangers, you must lift out the side pieces to access the top ends. Next, tin or lightly coat the hangers with 50/50 solder on both sides (photo 47). Brush and flux the came pieces at the top before inserting the hangers into their cavities (photo 48). Let the hangers cool longer than usual since brass takes longer to cool and solidify than some metals. Test the solder joints by pulling on each hanger with needle-nose pliers. If it feels firm and doesn't move, it will hold your panel. If not, solder it again, and let it cool.

You can also hang panels with heavy-gauge, tinned wire formed into a loop with twisted ends. These can be attached inside the came, as described above, or on the outside of the frame. Test your solder joint for strength after it cools.

Photo 48

Photo 47

The Projects

The following section presents a wide range of stained glass designs. As you thumb through, you'll find that the most complex pieces are placed at the end of this section. You may want to take these projects on as you become more accomplished.

If you find a project that you like, and want to begin there, you will have complete instructions. But keep in mind that you must learn the basics in the front of the book before beginning any project. Thumb back to a particular section when you need help during the process.

Each project is accompanied by a detailed template showing you how to cut the pieces apart. Enlarge it to the suggested finished size or to another size of your choice. If it is assembled with came or combines came and copper foil, the pieces are numbered to tell you the most practical order of assembly. If a project is constructed only of copper-foiled pieces, they are not numbered because you can assemble them in any order of your choice. Add your own numbering system to these pieces.

Each project also references two or more toolboxes under the heading of "tools and equipment." You'll find these lists on the following page. The basic toolbox contains all items (both tools and supplies) that you will routinely use to make the projects.

The glass colors that we used are listed, but keep in mind that you can change the palette of your pieces in any way that you like. You can also vary other factors such as the patina, the came that you use for your frame, or how you hang the piece. Again, we have merely suggested those things for your convenience.

Remember that learning stained glass takes some patience, especially when you're assembling, and this book will make the process as smooth as possible for you. For troubleshooting tips, refer to page 126. Most important, relax and have fun!

BASIC TOOLBOX & SUPPLIES

Heavy kraft paper
Carbon paper
Glass cutter and cutting fluid
Breaking pliers
Grozing pliers
Running pliers
Glass grinder with face shield and coolant
Light table (optional)
Flux, flux brush, and flux remover
Soldering iron, holder, and tip
Cleaning sponge
Wire brush
Glazing hammer and horseshoe nails
Waterproof marking pens in black, white and/or gold
Natural-bristle hand brush
Table brush and dust pan
Needle-nose pliers
Scissors
Wire cutters
Safety glasses
Safety gloves
Kitchen hot pad or oven glove
Non-ammonia based glass cleaner
Lint-free towels
Cotton-tipped swabs

LEAD TOOLBOX

Lead pattern shears
Lead vise and channel-lock pliers
Hacksaw (handsaw) with metal cutting blade
or electric came saw
Lead nippers (dykes)
Metal files

COPPER FOIL TOOLBOX

Foil pattern shears
Foil crimper or burnisher
Single-blade razor or craft knife

Bold Abstract Design

This striking piece incorporates came-wrapped nuggets. The design was originally used for the panels on a set of contemporary kitchen cabinets.

GLASS

Clear/textured

Amber/cathedral/textured

Burgundy/cathedral with clear swirls

Blue/cathedral with clear swirls

Large blue nugget (glob)

Medium amber nugget (glob)

TOOLS & EQUIPMENT

Basic toolbox and supplies

Lead toolbox

SUPPLIES

6 feet (1.8 m) of $7/32$-inch (.55 cm) H-channel lead came

5 feet (1.5 m) of $1/4$-inch (.64 cm) U-channel zinc came

50/50 solder

2 brass hangers

Black jack chain

Suggested finished size:
20 x 8 inches (50.8 x 20.3 cm)

INSTRUCTIONS

1. Enlarge the project template to the suggested finished size, and trace the pieces onto kraft paper. Trace the two nuggets onto the template in the places indicated to accurately record their size, and adjust the sizes of the surrounding pieces accordingly. Use the English method to cut and number each piece of glass.

2. Place the glass pieces on the template. Begin leading at the bottom left corner. Groze and grind the pieces to fit as you work.

3. When you reach the point of placing one of the nuggets, you'll need to wrap it first. Cut a piece of lead slightly longer than the nugget's circumference with a flat edge on one end. Place the flat edge of the lead strip on your work surface with the nugget in the channel, and begin rolling the lead around the edge of it, keeping it tight (photo 1). When the lead is wrapped as tightly as possible, mark and cut another flat edge and place the two flat ends together so they meet at the bottom (photo 2).

Photo 1

Photo 2

Photo 3

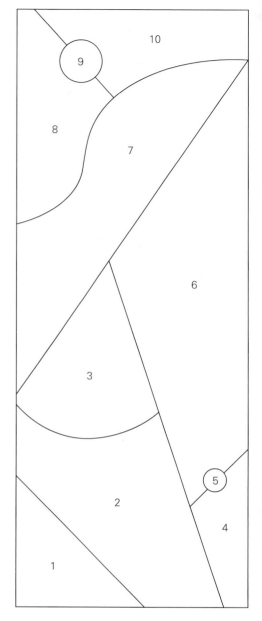

Press and roll this area on your work surface to round it off. Place the nugget by aligning the cut with one of the lead seams that crosses it. When you solder it in place, you'll be able to hide the cut (photo 3).

4. Continue leading until all the pieces are placed.

5. Use a saw to cut and miter the zinc came to fit around the piece as a frame/border. Hold the entire configuration (glass pieces and frame) in place with nails, making sure that everything fits. After this step, lift out each of the side pieces of the frame to add a hanger to the top. Tin the hangers, and solder them.

6. Clean all the lead joints before you flux and solder them. After soldering, remove all the nails. Clean off the flux residue. Carefully turn the panel over. Solder and clean the other side.

7. Polish the panel, cleaning the glass thoroughly.

8. Measure out a length of chain for hanging your piece. Open the link on one end, and attach it to one of the hangers. Close the link and secure it, then repeat this process on the other side.

Blue Rondel Design

Use rondels and bevels as accent pieces on a leaded panel to create interesting visual contrasts.

GLASS

Clear/textured
Cobalt blue/cathedral
2 blue rondels, each about 3 inches (7.6 cm) in diameter
Clear, oval-shaped bevel, 3 x 6 inches (7.6 x 15.3 cm)

TOOLS & EQUIPMENT

Basic toolbox and supplies
Lead toolbox

SUPPLIES

6 feet (1.8 m) of $7/32$-inch (.55 cm) H-channel lead came
6 feet (1.8 m) of $1/4$-inch (.64 cm) U-channel zinc came
50/50 solder
2 brass hangers
Silver-colored or black chain

Suggested finished size:
26 x 12 inches (66 x 30.5 cm)

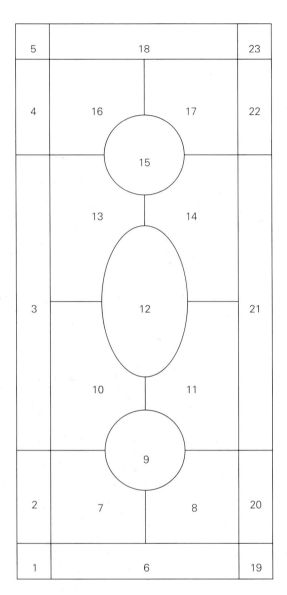

INSTRUCTIONS

1. Enlarge the project template to the suggested finished size. Because the rondels and bevels can vary in shape, trace them onto the enlarged template where they belong, and mark the top center of each glass piece for later reference.

2. If all of your glass is fairly transparent, use the English cutting method to cut out the pieces. If the blue rondels are fairly dark, use the cut-apart pattern method (with lead pattern shears) instead. Be sure to number your pieces as you cut them.

3. Turn the template 90° so that the first five pattern pieces are closest to you. Position the glass pieces on the template. Use lead bumpers to assist you as you begin leading in the bottom right corner. Pay attention to the pattern, making sure to keep the long vertical came pieces whole. (Don't be tempted to break them up with pieces that cross them as you assemble.) Groze or grind the glass pieces to fit as you work.

4. Wrap the bevel and rondels with came as described in the project on page 45. Use the marks made in step 1 as your beginning point for wrapping. After these pieces are wrapped, position them during assembly without soldering them. Simply nail them in place. Align any cut in the surrounding came with a lead seam that crosses it. When you solder later, you'll be able to hide the seam.

5. Use a saw to cut and miter the zinc came to fit around the piece as a frame/border. Hold the entire configuration (glass pieces and frame) in place with nails, making sure that everything fits. After this step, lift out each of the side pieces of the frame to add a hanger to the top. Tin the hangers, and solder them.

6. Clean all the lead joints before you flux and solder them. After soldering, remove all the nails. Clean off the flux residue. Carefully turn the panel over. Solder and clean the other side.

7. Polish the panel, cleaning the glass thoroughly.

8. Measure out a length of chain for hanging your piece. Open the link on one end, and attach it to one of the hangers. Close the link and secure it, then repeat this process on the other hanger.

Art Glass Panel

One-of-a-kind glass draws attention to the center of this piece,
while long lines of lead lend it physical strength.

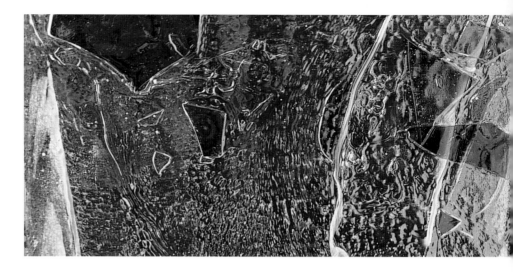

GLASS

Clear/textured

Soft lavender/cathedral

Art glass (one-of-a-kind piece of glass)

TOOLS & EQUIPMENT

Basic toolbox and supplies

Lead toolbox

SUPPLIES

6 feet (1.8 m) of 7/32-inch (.55 cm) H-channel lead came

5 feet (1.5 m) of 1/4-inch (.64 cm) U-channel zinc came

50/50 solder

2 brass hangers

Silver-colored jack chain

Suggested finished size:
12 1/2 x 16 inches
(30.5 x 40.6 cm)

INSTRUCTIONS

1. Enlarge the project template to the suggested finished size. Use either method of cutting (cut-apart pattern with lead pattern shears or English method) to cut out and number the glass pieces, depending on the opacity of the glass. Position the glass pieces on the template.

2. Begin the process of leading in the bottom left corner as shown on the template, working up the side of the panel to deal with each vertical line.

3. Groze and grind the pieces as needed during assembly, keeping the lines straight. Work up the edge of the panel, through the center, and then finally to the upper right corner until all the pieces are leaded and square.

4. Use a saw to cut and miter the zinc came to fit around the piece as a frame/border. Hold the entire configuration (glass pieces and frame) in place with nails, making sure that everything fits. After this step, lift out each of the side pieces of the frame to add a hanger to the top. Tin the hangers, and solder them.

5. Clean all the joints before fluxing and soldering them. After soldering, remove any nails, and clean off the flux residue. Turn the panel, and repeat these steps on the other side.

6. Polish the panel, cleaning the glass thoroughly.

7. Measure out a length of chain for hanging your piece. Open the link on one end and attach it to one of the hangers. Close the link and secure it, and then repeat on the other side.

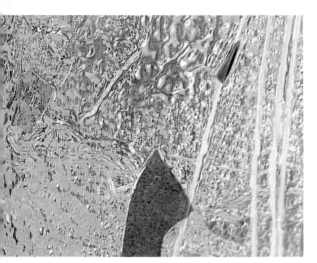

8	9		23	24	25	26	27
7			22				
6	10	12	15		16	21	
5			13	14		20	
			11			19	
4						18	
1	2	3				17	

Victorian Tulip

This small piece shows you how to negotiate curves on a leaded panel.

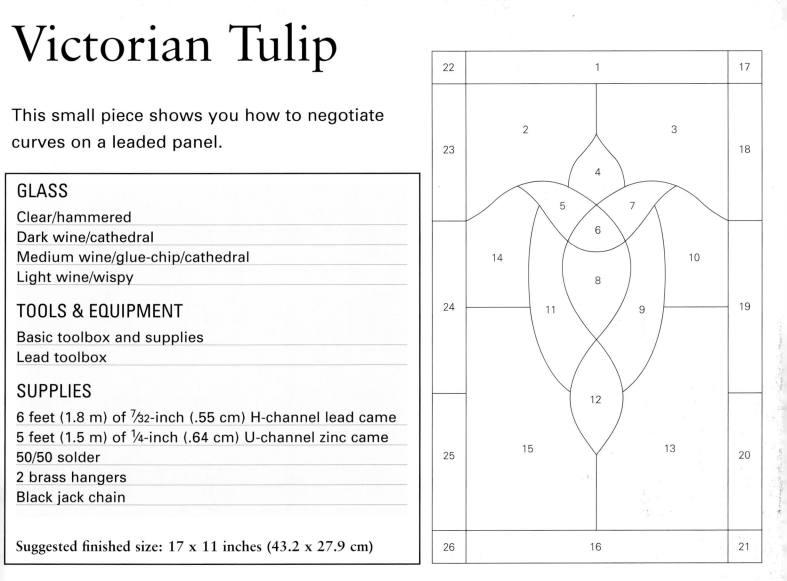

GLASS

Clear/hammered
Dark wine/cathedral
Medium wine/glue-chip/cathedral
Light wine/wispy

TOOLS & EQUIPMENT

Basic toolbox and supplies
Lead toolbox

SUPPLIES

6 feet (1.8 m) of $7/32$-inch (.55 cm) H-channel lead came
5 feet (1.5 m) of $1/4$-inch (.64 cm) U-channel zinc came
50/50 solder
2 brass hangers
Black jack chain

Suggested finished size: 17 x 11 inches (43.2 x 27.9 cm)

INSTRUCTIONS

1. Enlarge the project template to the suggested finished size. Depending on the opacity of your glass, use the English cutting method or cut-apart pattern method (with lead pattern shears) to cut out and number each piece of glass.

2. Turn the template upside down on your work surface so that you begin working at the top of the piece. Position the glass pieces on the template. Use lead bumpers to assist you as you begin assembling the pieces with lead. Groze and grind the glass to fit the pattern.

3. Follow the instructions on pages 36 to 39 for specifics about assembling this piece.

4. Use a saw to cut and miter the zinc came to fit around the piece as a frame/border. Hold the entire configuration (glass pieces and frame) in place with nails, making sure that everything fits. After this step, lift out each side of the frame to add a hanger to the top of the came. Tin the hangers, and solder them.

5. Clean all the lead joints before you flux and solder them. After soldering, remove all the nails. Clean off the flux residue. Carefully turn over the panel. Solder and clean the other side.

6. Polish the panel, cleaning the glass thoroughly.

7. Measure out a length of chain for hanging your piece. Open the link on one end, and attach it to one of the hangers. Close the link and secure it, then repeat this process on the other side.

Clear Textures Panel

The combination of clear bevels and textured glass in this panel creates a sophisticated look.

GLASS

2-inch-square (5 x 5 cm) clear bevel

9 clear bevels, each 1 inch square (2.5 x 2.5 cm)

Assorted clear/textured

TOOLS & EQUIPMENT

Basic toolbox and supplies

Lead toolbox

SUPPLIES

5 feet (1.5 m) of $7/32$-inch (.55 cm) H-channel lead came

6 feet (1.8 m) of $1/4$-inch (.64 cm) U-channel zinc came

50/50 solder

2 brass hangers

Black jack chain

Suggested finished size: 20 x 9 inches (50.8 x 22.9 cm)

INSTRUCTIONS

1. Enlarge the template to the suggested finished size. Position and place the bevels to make sure that they fit the pattern exactly. If they don't, adjust the lines as needed before you cut the surrounding pieces of glass. Use the English method to cut and number each piece of glass from the template. Position the glass pieces on the template.

2. Use lead bumpers to assist you as you begin leading at the bottom and work upward, adding the square bevels as you go. Grind and groze the pieces as needed to fit them into the came.

3. Use a saw to cut and miter the zinc came to fit around the piece as a frame/border. Hold the entire configuration (glass pieces and frame) in place with nails, making sure that everything fits. After this step, lift out each of the side pieces of the frame to add a hanger to the top. Tin the hangers, and solder them.

4. Clean all the lead joints before you flux and solder them. After soldering, remove all the nails. Clean off the flux residue. Carefully turn over the panel. Solder and clean the other side.

5. Polish the panel, cleaning the glass thoroughly.

6. Measure out a length of chain for hanging your piece. Open the link on one end, and attach it to one of the hangers. Close the link and secure it, then repeat this process on the other side.

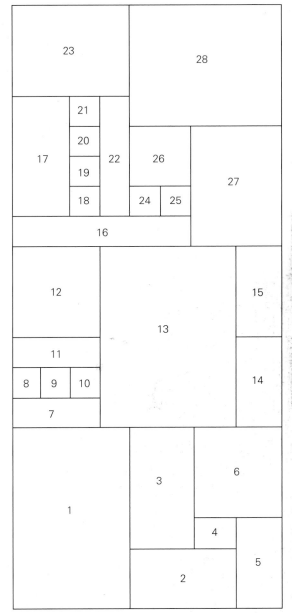

Black Iridescent Panel

This unique piece makes the most of both sides of iridescent glass. By reversing certain pieces, you'll create contrasts in the design. The resulting panel is interesting when viewed from either side.

GLASS

Black iridescent, 36-inch-square (91.4 x 91.4 cm) piece

TOOLS & EQUIPMENT

Basic toolbox and supplies

Lead toolbox

SUPPLIES

2 lengths of $7/32$-inch (.55 cm) H-channel lead came, each 6 feet (1.8 m) long

6 feet (1.8 m) of $1/4$-inch (.64 cm) U-channel zinc came

50/50 solder

2 brass hangers

Black jack chain

Suggested finished size: 23 x 12½ inches (58.4 x 31.8 cm)

INSTRUCTIONS

1. Enlarge the project template to the suggested finished size. Trace the pieces onto kraft paper, and cut them apart with lead pattern shears.

2. Take a look at the finished piece. About a third of the glass pieces shown are dark black, while the others shown have an iridescent surface. On the other side of the panel, the effect is reversed. To create the contrasting pieces of glass, you simply need to flip over/reverse selected pattern pieces before tracing them on the plain side of the glass with a light-colored marking pen. (The pieces that we reversed are indicated in the shaded areas on the template.)

3. Cut and number the glass pieces. Position them on your template, reversing some as planned.

4. Begin the leading process in the lower left corner, stacking the pieces as shown, cutting angled joints in the came as needed. Then, move to the bottom of the piece and work across and up. Continue to follow the sequence carefully. Grind and groze the glass edges to fit into the lead.

5. Use a saw to cut and miter the zinc came to fit around the piece as a frame/border. Hold the entire configuration (glass pieces and frame) in place with nails, making sure that everything fits. After this step, lift out each side of the frame to add a hanger to the top of the came. Tin the hangers, and solder them.

6. Clean all the lead joints before you flux and solder them. After soldering, remove all the nails. Clean off the flux residue. Carefully turn over the panel. Solder and clean the other side.

7. Polish the panel, cleaning the glass thoroughly.

8. Measure out a length of chain for hanging your piece. Open the link on one end, and attach it to one of the hangers. Close the link and secure it, then repeat this process on the other side.

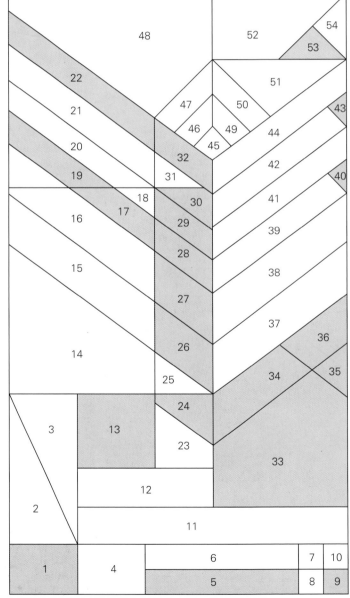

Classic Geometric Design with Bevels

This design combines subtle green glass with clear bevels for an elegant look.

GLASS

Light green/opalescent

Clear/textured

2 bevels, each 2 inches
square (5.1 x 5.1 cm)

2 bevels, each 1½ inches
square (3.8 x 3.8 cm)

TOOLS & EQUIPMENT

Basic toolbox and supplies

Lead toolbox

SUPPLIES

6 feet (1.8 m) of 7/32-inch
(.55 cm) H-channel lead came

5 feet (1.5 m) of ¼-inch
(.64 cm) U-channel zinc came

50/50 solder

2 brass hangers

Silver-colored chain

Suggested finished size:
20 x 8 inches (50.8 x 20.3 cm)

INSTRUCTIONS

1. Enlarge the project template to the suggested finished size. Trace it on to kraft paper, and cut the pieces apart with lead pattern shears. Cut out and number the glass pieces.

2. Begin by leading the bottom central piece, grozing and grinding pieces as needed to make them fit. Work up and through the center before adding the side pieces. Keep vertical lines in whole came lengths.

3. Use a saw to cut and miter the zinc came to fit around the piece as a frame/border. Hold the entire configuration (glass pieces and frame) in place with nails, making sure that everything fits. After this is determined, lift out each of the side pieces of the frame to add a hanger to the top. Tin the hangers, and solder them.

4. Clean all the lead joints before you flux and solder them. After soldering, remove all the nails. Clean off the flux residue. Carefully turn the panel over. Solder and clean the other side.

5. Polish the panel, cleaning the glass thoroughly.

6. Measure out a length of chain for hanging your piece. Open the link on one end, and attach it to one of the hangers. Close the link and secure it, then repeat this process on the other side.

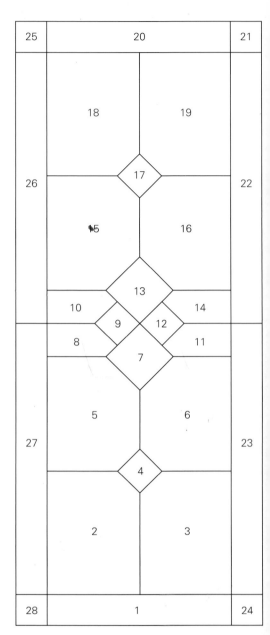

Floating Ribbon Design

This project combines leading and copper foiling. The heavy, structural lines are leaded; the lighter, undulating lines are foiled.

GLASS

Clear/swirled

Light champagne and clear/swirled

Light teal and clear/swirled

TOOLS & EQUIPMENT

Basic toolbox and supplies

Lead toolbox

Copper foil toolbox

SUPPLIES

6 feet (1.8 m) of $7/32$-inch (.55 cm) H-channel lead came

5 feet (1.5 m) of ¼-inch (.64 cm) U-channel zinc came

$3/16$-inch (.48 cm) and $7/32$-inch (.55 cm) black-backed copper foil

50/50 and 60/40 solder

Black patina

2 brass hangers

Silver-colored jack chain

Suggested finished size: 12 x 16 inches (30.5 x 40.6 cm)

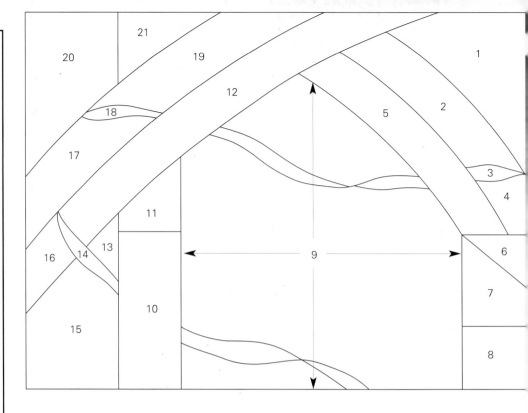

INSTRUCTIONS

1. Enlarge the project template to the suggested finished size. Use the English method to cut out the glass pieces. Groze and grind the pieces as needed to fit the template.

2. Flip the template on your work surface so that the right side is closest to you. Take a look at the pattern and study it for a moment.

The smaller ribbon-shaped pieces will be copper-foiled, while the larger pieces will be leaded.

3. Grind the smaller pieces resembling ribbons, foil them, and position them on the template. Solder together the largest central piece of glass and the ribbons above and below this piece, leaving the edges of this unit exposed (no foil). (See page 39 for more information on combining copper foil and lead.) After this, high-bead both sides of the copper-foiled unit up to the edges. Allow room for the lead to overlap.

4. Lead the first few pieces as numbered, laying in this foiled unit when you reach it.

5. Continue leading the left side, laying the small foiled sections, combine them with the leaded ones.

6. When you complete the leading, add the zinc came frame.

7. Clean the came joints, then flux and solder them. Tack-solder all the foiled pieces to the lead came with 50/50 solder. Flat-fill the remaining foiled pieces with 50/50 solder, followed by 60/40 solder for high-beading. Tack-solder the remaining lead came. Clean off the flux residue, and turn the panel over. Repeat the cleaning, fluxing, and soldering.

8. Clean off the flux residue. Apply black patina to the copper-foiled solder seams.

9. Measure out a length of chain for hanging your piece. Open the link on one end and attach it to one of the hangers. Close the link and secure it, and then repeat on the other side.

Repeating Pattern Design

This project shows you how to repeat a template to make an interesting design. The separate copper-foiled panels are leaded together with copper came.

GLASS

Clear/textured

Bronze/cathedral

TOOLS & EQUIPMENT

Basic toolbox and supplies

Copper foil toolbox

Long wooden ruler or ¼-inch
(6.4 cm) lattice strip

SUPPLIES

2 lengths of ⁷⁄₃₂-inch (.55 cm)
H-channel copper came, each
6 feet (1.8 m) long

⁷⁄₃₂-inch (.55 cm) copper foil

50/50 and 60/40 solder

18-gauge copper wire

Copper patina for solder

Copper jack chain

Suggested finished size:
30 x 7½ inches (76.2 x 19.1 cm)

INSTRUCTIONS

1. Enlarge the project template to the suggested finished size. Use the English method to cut and number three identical pieces of glass from each pattern piece. When you cut the long background pieces, use several progressive curved score lines to break out the deep curves. Groze and grind the pieces to fit the template.

2. Position one set of pieces on the template, and apply copper foil to each piece, leaving the outer edges unfoiled. Flux, tack-solder, and flat-fill the interior foiled lines with 50/50 solder. High-bead the seams with 60/40 solder. Clean off the flux residue. Carefully turn the panel over, and repeat on the other side.

3. Foil and solder the remaining two panels in the same way.

4. Cut one of the long pieces of copper came in half. On your work surface, nail the long wooden ruler or lattice strip into your work table along the outer edge. Align the came with the wooden piece, channel side in, so that it won't slide as you work.

5. Slide one of the panels into the top of the came, and shore up the other sides with came bumpers.

6. Measure and cut two pieces of came the width of the panel to serve as the two interior horizontal pieces. Assemble the remaining two panels along the long came with these pieces between them.

7. Cut the top, bottom, and remaining side piece from the came to complete the frame, mitering the edges to fit around the panel.

8. Clean the came joints, then flux and solder them. Tack-solder the top and bottom centers of the panels to the copper came. Clean off the flux residue and remove the nails. Turn the panel over and solder the other side, repeating the same steps.

9. Hold the piece up on its long edge in a vertical position. Solder an 18-gauge wire twist for hanging to the outer side of the top edge. Clean off the flux residue. Repeat this process on the other side, adding another wire twist hanger.

10. Measure out a length of chain for hanging your piece. Open the link on one end and attach it to one of the hangers. Close the link and secure it, and then repeat on the other side.

Falling Leaves Panel

The length of this copper-foiled panel accentuates the gentle, down-ward movement of the leaves.

GLASS

Clear/textured

Gold seedy/cathedral

Green with gold
seedy/cathedral

Green seedy/cathedral

Red and gold seedy/
cathedral

TOOLS & EQUIPMENT

Basic toolbox and supplies

Copper foil toolbox

SUPPLIES

2 lengths of ¼-inch (.64 cm)
U-channel zinc came, each
6 feet (1.8 m) long

³⁄₁₆-inch(.48 cm) and ⅞-inch
(.55 cm) black-backed
copper foil

50/50 and 60/40 solder

2 brass hangers

Black patina made
for solder

Black patina made for zinc

Black jack chain

**Suggested finished size: 36 x 8
inches (91.4 x 20.3 cm)**

INSTRUCTIONS

1. Enlarge the template to the
suggested finished size. Trace the
pieces onto kraft paper, and cut
them out with copper foil pattern
shears. Cut out and number the
glass pieces. Groze and grind them
to fit the pattern in preparation for
foiling.

2. Apply copper foil to the pieces,
and position them on the template.

3. Apply flux close to the outer
edges, then tack-solder the pieces
together with 50/50 solder. Leave a
small margin around the edges to
allow for the zinc came frame as
you solder. Flux, tack-solder, and
flat-fill the inner seams with 50/50
solder, then high-bead with 60/40
solder. Clean off the flux residue.

4. Use a saw to cut and miter the
zinc came to fit around the piece as
frame/border. Hold the entire configuration (glass pieces and frame)
in place with nails, making sure that
everything fits and is square. After
this step, lift out each side of the
frame to add a hanger to the top of
the came. Tin the hangers, and solder them.

5. Clean the zinc at the corners and
where the foiled seams meet it. Flux
and solder the corner seams, and
tack-solder the foiled pieces to the
zinc frame along the border. Clean
off the flux residue. Turn over
the panel.

6. Solder the panel's reverse side.
Clean off the flux residue.

7. Apply the black patina made for
solder to the solder seams. Use the
wire brush to clean the zinc came,
then apply the black patina made
for zinc to both sides.

8. Polish the panel, cleaning the
glass thoroughly.

9. Measure out a length of chain for
hanging your piece. Open the link
on one end, and attach it to one of
the hangers. Close the link and
secure it, then repeat this process
on the other side.

Magical Geode Panel

This unusual abstract piece combines leading with copper-foiled geodes and nuggets.

GLASS

Clear/textured

Swirled red and clear

Several cut and polished geodes, about $\frac{7}{32}$-inch (.55 cm) thick

Several red and amber medium-size nuggets (globs)

4 dark purple glass tiles or cut squares of purple glass, each 1 inch square (2.5 x 2.5 cm)

TOOLS & EQUIPMENT

Basic toolbox and supplies

Lead toolbox

Copper foil toolbox

SUPPLIES

6 feet (1.8 m) of $\frac{7}{32}$-inch (.55 cm) H-channel lead came

5 feet (1.5 m) of $\frac{1}{4}$-inch (.64 cm) U-channel zinc came

3 mm (.062-inch-thick) brass or copper shim, 12-inch-square (30.5 x 30.5 cm) piece

$\frac{7}{32}$-inch (.55 cm) and $\frac{1}{4}$-inch (.64 cm) black-backed copper foil

50/50 and 60/40 solder

2 brass hangers

Black jack chain

Suggested finished size: 16 x 10 inches (40.6 x 25.4 cm)

INSTRUCTIONS

1. Enlarge the project template to the size indicated. Trace the pattern onto kraft paper, and cut it apart with lead pattern shears. Set aside the two pattern pieces to be used for the brass shim indicated by the shaded area on the pattern.

2. Use the other pattern pieces to cut and number each piece of glass. Groze and grind the edges as needed to fit the template.

3. Trace the two shim patterns onto the brass sheeting with a marker, and cut them out with the scissors or metal shears.

4. Position the pieces on the template, and begin leading in the bottom left corner, assembling pieces in the order suggested on the template. Stop after you've added pieces 11 and 12.

5. Arrange the geodes and nuggets in a freeform pattern on the two pieces of shim. Once the pieces are placed, trace around them with a black marker. Use metal shears or scissors to cut out the holes in the brass for the embellishments to fit. (You'll have to cut a line over to each circular hole to extract the piece. These lines will be covered with soldering later.) If the shim is tarnished, clean it with a wire brush or brass wool.

6. Place the edges of the shim into the lead as you would pieces of glass. Grind smooth edges on the nuggets so that they fit into the holes. Foil the nuggets and geodes, and place them in the shim. Lead the upper edge of the shim. Lead the rest of the glass pieces as numbered on the template.

7. Use a saw to cut and miter the zinc came to fit around the piece as a frame/border. Hold the entire configuration (glass pieces and frame) in place with nails, making sure that everything fits and the frame is square. After this step, lift out each side of the frame to add a hanger to the top of the came. Tin the hangers, and solder them.

8. Clean all the lead joints before you flux and solder them. Flux the foiled stones and glass nuggets before soldering them to the brass shim.

9. Lightly flux the surface of the shim. Slowly apply a thin coat of solder to the brass, developing texture by applying heavier amounts to some areas. The metal will absorb heat easily and cool down slowly, so you'll have to work slowly.

10. After soldering, remove all the nails. Clean off the flux residue. Carefully turn the panel over. Solder and clean the back as you did the front (photo 1).

11. Polish the panel, cleaning the glass thoroughly.

12. Measure out a length of chain for hanging your piece. Open the link on one end, and attach it to one of the hangers. Close the link and secure it, then repeat this process on the other side.

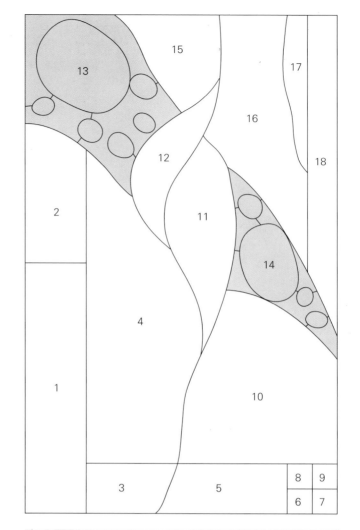

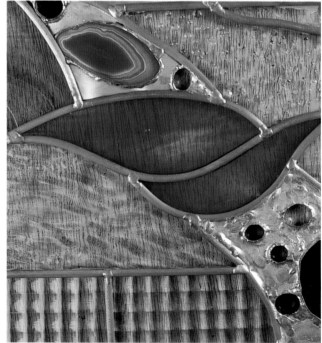

Photo 1

70

Yin-Yang Design

This panel was created from scraps of clear textured glass and various bevels to make a patchwork of textures.
If you can't find the exact bevels we used, improvise with others, adjusting the design as needed.

GLASS

1 x 10-inch (2.5 x 25.4 cm) bevel

2 x 4-inch (5.1 x 10.2 cm) bevel

1½ x 3-inch (3.8 x 7.6 cm) bevel

2-inch (5.1 cm) semi-circular bevel

1½ x 3-inch (3.8 x 7.6 cm) curved corner bevel

2 tear-shaped bevels, each 2½ x 4 inches (6.4 x 10.2 cm)

Clear textured glass scraps of your choice, such as frosted, rippled, or wavy

TOOLS & EQUIPMENT

Basic toolbox and supplies

Copper foil toolbox

SUPPLIES

4 feet (1.2 m) of ¼-inch (.64 cm) U-channel zinc came

3/16-inch (4.8 cm) silver-backed copper foil

50/50 and 60/40 solder

2 brass hangers

Silver-colored jack chain

Suggested finished size:
10 x 8 inches (25.4 x 20.3 cm)

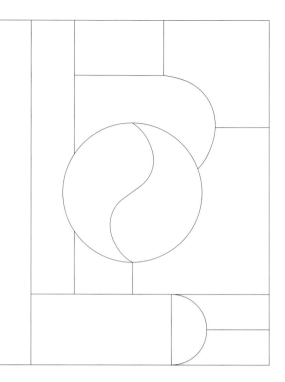

INSTRUCTIONS

1. Enlarge the template to the size indicated. Position the bevels on the template. If they vary in size from the template, change the template lines to accommodate them.

2. Use the English method to cut out the textured glass pieces using a variety of clear glass pieces of your choice. Groze and grind the pieces to fit the template.

3. Foil all the inside seams of the design, overlapping the foil slightly on the outer edges that will be covered later with the zinc came frame.

4. Position the foiled pieces on the template. Apply flux and tack-solder the outer seams to hold the pieces in place. Flux and flat-fill all the seams with 50/50 solder. High-bead the seams with 60/40 solder, allowing room around the outer edge for the zinc came. Turn over the panel, and solder the back in the same manner.

5. Use a saw to cut and miter the zinc came to fit around the piece as a frame/border. Hold the entire configuration (glass pieces and frame) in place with nails, making sure that everything fits. After this step, lift out each side of the frame to add a hanger to the top of the came. Tin the hangers, and solder them.

6. Clean all the came joints before you flux and solder them. Solder the corners and all seams that meet the outer came frame. Clean off the flux residue.

7. Polish the panel, cleaning the glass thoroughly.

8. Measure out a length of chain for hanging your piece. Open the link on one end, and attach it to one of the hangers. Close the link and secure it, then repeat this process on the other side.

Ice
Crystal
Panel

This design
demonstrates
how you can create
subtle, interesting
effects by changing
the grain direction of
textured glass. The
fluted glass pieces are
cut to follow the lines
and curves of
the emblem.

GLASS

Clear/crystal

Narrow fluted or ribbed
piece of glass

TOOLS & EQUIPMENT

Basic toolbox and supplies

Lead toolbox

Long wooden ruler or
¼-inch (.64 cm) lattice strip

SUPPLIES

2 lengths of ⁷/₃₂-inch (.55 cm)
H-channel lead came, each
6 feet (1.8 m) long

2 lengths of ⅜-inch (.95 cm)
U-channel zinc came, each 6
feet (1.8 m) long

50/50 solder

2 brass hangers

Silver-colored jack chain

Suggested finished size:
26 x 16 inches (66 x 40.6 cm)

INSTRUCTIONS

1. Enlarge the template to the suggested finished size. Use the English method to cut out and number the panel pieces, paying attention to the direction of the grain on the fluted pieces and varying the background pieces of textured glass as you wish.

2. Turn the template sideways so that you can begin assembly along the left side (note the numbers on the template). Position the long ruler or lattice strip along the long border line, and nail it to your table to help keep the pieces aligned during assembly.

3. Begin leading along this line, keeping the horizontal lines matched even. When setting the thicker fluted glass pieces, tap them gently into the lead with the rubber head of a glazing hammer.

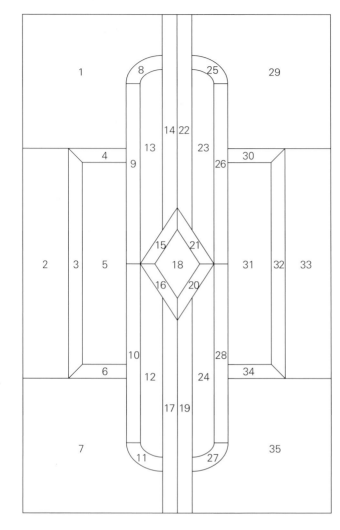

4. Use a saw to cut and miter the pieces of zinc came to form the frame. Hold the entire configuration (glass pieces and frame) in place with nails, making sure that everything fits. After this step, lift out each side of the frame to add a hanger to the top of the came. Tin the hangers, and solder them.

5. Clean all the lead joints before you flux and solder them. After soldering, remove all the nails. Clean off the flux residue. Carefully turn over the panel. Solder and clean the other side.

6. Polish the panel, cleaning the glass thoroughly.

7. Measure out a length of chain for hanging your piece. Open the link on one end, and attach it to one of the hangers. Close the link and secure it, then repeat this process on the other side.

Egyptian Fan Design

The larger pieces of glass that comprise this design make it bold and impressive. Because of the size of the pieces, we recommend that you cement the panel as a final step.

GLASS

Champagne and
white/translucent

Champagne and white/wispy

Teal and white/translucent

Teal/glue-chip/cathedral

TOOLS & EQUIPMENT

Basic toolbox and supplies

Lead toolbox

SUPPLIES

2 lengths of $7/32$-inch (.55 cm)
H-channel lead came, each 6
feet (1.8 m) long

2 lengths of $3/8$-inch (.95 cm)
U-channel zinc came, each 6
feet (1.8 m) long

50/50 solder

2 brass hangers

Black jack chain

Cement or glazing compound

Whiting

**Suggested finished size: 24 inches
square (61 x 61 cm)**

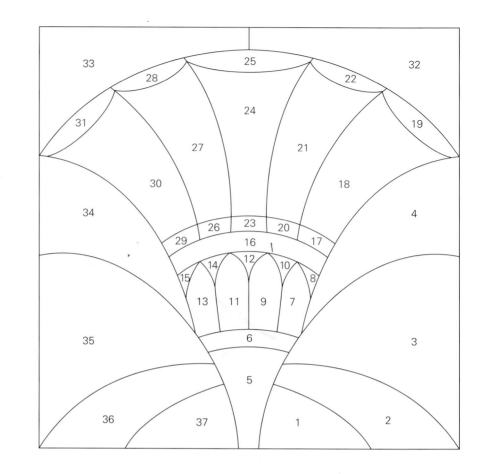

INSTRUCTIONS

1. Enlarge the template to the suggested finished size. Trace the pieces onto the kraft paper, and use lead pattern shears to cut out the pattern pieces. After you cut out and number the glass pieces, position them on the template.

2. Begin leading from the bottom right side as indicated by the numbers on the template. (Notice that you're first putting in pieces on the right side that will serve to support the curved fan pieces that will rest

against these pieces.) Groze and grind the pieces to fit the came as needed.

3. Continue leading by moving from the bottom of the fan design and up through the center before moving to the top. Add right and left outer pieces next, followed by the bottom right side pieces.

4. Use a saw to cut and miter the pieces of zinc came that fit around the frame. Hold the entire configuration (glass pieces and frame) in place with nails, making sure that everything fits and is square. After this step, lift out each side of the frame to add a hanger to the top of the came. Tin the hangers, and solder them.

5. Clean all the lead joints before you flux and solder them. After soldering, remove all the nails. Clean off the flux residue. Carefully turn the panel over. Solder and clean the other side.

6. Apply cement or glazing compound to the panel to add strength to it, and clean it with whiting (see pages 14 to 16). Let it cure for 24 to 48 hours.

7. Measure out a length of chain for hanging your piece. Open the link on one end, and attach it to one of the hangers. Close the link and secure it, then repeat this process on the other side.

Prairie
Gold
Panel

To complement the glass color palette, this project features bright brass-capped lead and brass came.

GLASS

Light gold/cathedral
Medium gold/cathedral
Dark brown/cathedral/textured

TOOLS & EQUIPMENT

Basic toolbox and supplies
Lead toolbox

SUPPLIES

2 lengths of $7/32$-inch (.55 cm)
H-channel brass-capped lead
came, each 6-foot (1.8 m) long
6 feet (1.8 m) of $3/8$-inch
(.95 cm) U-channel brass came
50/50 solder
2 brass hangers
Gold paint pen
Brass or gold-colored
jack chain

**Suggested finished size: 25 x 13
inches (63.5 x 33 cm)**

INSTRUCTIONS

1. Enlarge the project template to the suggested finished size. If all of your glass pieces are fairly transparent, use the English cutting method. If your brown glass is too dark, use the cut-apart pattern method instead. Cut and number each piece of glass.

2. Before you begin leading, you might need to use a saw to cut several small pieces of the brass-capped lead off for use as bumpers. Or, if you have lead scraps around that are the same size as the brass-capped lead, you can use those pieces instead.

3. Position the glass pieces on the template. Begin leading in the bottom left corner, cutting the brass-capped pieces with the saw as you fit them into place. You'll stack and align certain pieces against the long vertical lines.

4. When all glass pieces are in place, cut and miter four pieces of brass came for the panel's frame. Hold the entire configuration (glass pieces and frame) in place with nails, making sure that everything fits. After this step, lift out each side of the frame to add a hanger to the top of the came. Tin the bottom of the two hangers, leaving the brass top exposed.

5. Clean all the joints, then flux and tack-solder them. Brass absorbs more heat than lead does, so solder slowly to create solid joints. After soldering, remove all the nails. Clean off the flux residue. Carefully turn over the panel. Solder and clean the other side.

6. Use the gold paint pen to color the soldered joints to match the brass. Carefully turn the panel over and repeat on the other side.

7. Polish the panel, cleaning the glass thoroughly.

8. Measure out a length of chain for hanging your piece. Open the link on one end, and attach it to one of the hangers. Close the link and secure it, then repeat this process on the other side.

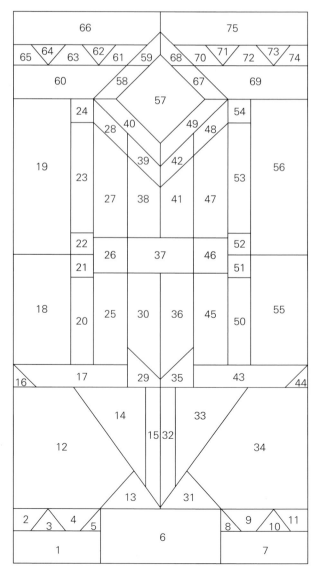

Street Address Sign

Begin with the basic template shown, then add your own street numbers. You'll cement the border pieces to prepare the piece for hanging outside, and frame it with wood.

GLASS

Clear/glue-chipped

Blue streaky/opaque

White/opaque

TOOLS & EQUIPMENT

Basic toolbox and supplies

Lead toolbox

Copper foil toolbox

SUPPLIES

6 feet (1.8 m) of ¼-inch (.64 cm) H-channel lead came

6 feet (1.8 m) of ⅜-inch (.95 cm) U-channel zinc came

7/32-inch (.55 cm) black-backed copper foil

50/50 and 60/40 solder

Black patina for solder

Cement or glazing compound (for edges)

Whiting (for edges)

Painted wooden frame made to fit around piece

Several screw eyes

Silver-colored jack chain

Suggested finished size:
12 x 24 inches (30.5 x 61 cm)

INSTRUCTIONS

1. Enlarge the template to the suggested finished size. In the center area, we've indicated how we drew and cut the numbers "515." Study these numbers, as well as the other examples, to see how surrounding cut lines are used to fit the pieces together. Emulate this method for your numbers, making small thumbnail sketches to work out the best design. If you wish, you can draw the design small and enlarge it to fit on top of the template before tracing it along with the surrounding pieces.

2. After you've created the template, trace the pattern pieces on kraft paper and cut them out with copper foil pattern shears. Cut out and number the glass pieces.

3. Apply black-backed copper foil to all the pieces of the inner section (numbers and rectangular designs on either side), leaving the outer edges free so that they can be fitted into lead came.

4. Position the foiled pieces on the template. Flux and tack-solder the outer edges with 50/50 solder. Flat-fill the inner seams with 50/50 solder, then high-bead them with 60/40 solder. When you solder, remember to leave an allowance for the came to overlap around the outer edges.

5. Lead the border pieces in the order shown on the template. The two vertical border lines on either end are formed by unbroken pieces of came. This means that you'll be working with two short pieces of came on either end to complete the long horizontal lines that cross these vertical lines.

6. Use a saw to cut and miter the zinc came to fit around the piece as a border. Hold the entire configuration (glass pieces and frame) in place with nails, making sure that everything fits.

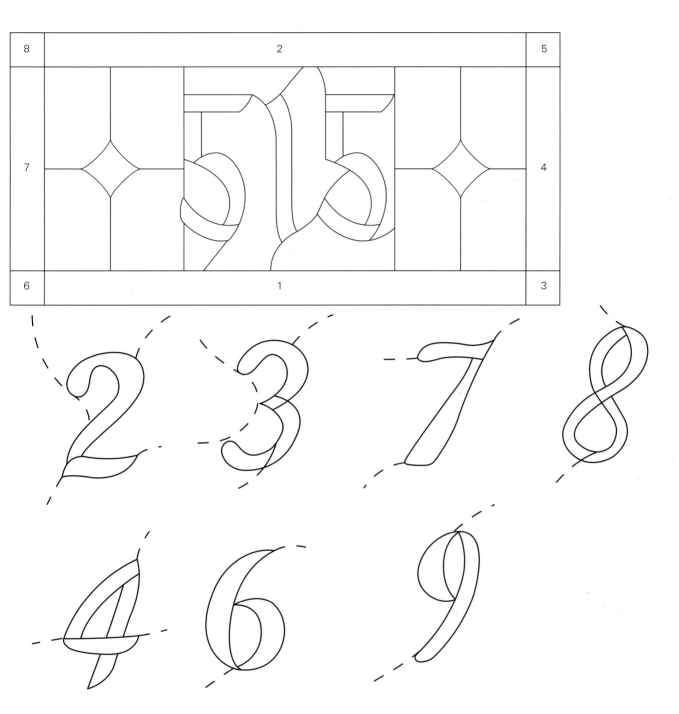

7. Clean the lead and zinc came joints, then flux and solder them. Tack-solder the areas where the foiled pieces touch the came. Clean off the flux residue.

8. Turn the piece over and solder the back. Clean off the flux residue.

9. Apply cement or glazing compound and whiting (see pages 14 to 16) to the leaded border pieces. Repeat on the front side and allow to cure.

10. Apply black patina to the soldered seams.

11. Position the piece in the wooden frame, and use small nails other hardware to secure it.

12. Add screw eyes to the top of the frame.

13. Measure a length of chain for hanging, and open the link at one end. Attach it to the screw eye by closing the link. Repeat on the other side.

Arts and Craft Lamp

By replicating a pattern four times, you'll create the sides of this gorgeous shade. When you buy the glass for this piece, make sure to quadruple the amount.

INSTRUCTIONS

1. Enlarge the template to the suggested finished size. Trace the pattern onto kraft paper, and cut it apart with copper foil pattern shears. On the glass, trace and number four of each of the pattern pieces. Cut out all the pieces. Groze and grind them to fit the pattern. Make certain that the sides are very straight and even.

2. Foil one set of glass pieces, and position it on the template. Nail down the two wooden rulers along each angled side edge. You'll use this jig each time you assemble a side, aligning the pieces so that they come out even.

3. Flux and tack-solder near the outer edges of the first set of pieces with 50/50 solder. Continue to tack and flat-fill the inner seams, leaving the edges unsoldered. High-bead the inner seams with 60/40 solder. Clean off the flux residue. Turn over the panel, being careful not to disturb the outer foiled edges. Solder the inner back seams as you did the front. Clean off the flux residue, and set aside the first panel.

4. Foil and solder the remaining three panels, following steps 2 and 3. Clean the glass thoroughly without disturbing the foil on the outer edges.

5. Apply patina to the inner solder seams on both the front and back of each of the four panels. Clear your work surface by removing the rulers and template.

6. Place the four panels approximately ⅛ inch (.3 cm) apart on the work surface as shown in figure 1 (page 85). Overlap the adjacent edges with short pieces of electrical tape, as shown. Press the tape down firmly on the clean glass without pressing down heavily on the copper foiled edges. On the end of the fourth panel, attach two extra pieces of tape, leaving an end extended to join back on the first panel when in place.

7. On another part of your work surface, nail down the other two wooden rulers at a 90° angle. This configuration will help you square the panels as they're lifted up in the next step.

GLASS

Beige and white/opaque

Gold/cathedral

Gold and brown/cathedral

4 bevels, each 1½ inches square (3.8 x 3.8 cm)

TOOLS & EQUIPMENT

Basic toolbox and supplies

Copper foil toolbox

SUPPLIES

7/32-inch (.55 cm) copper foil

4 long wooden rulers or ¼-inch (.64 mm) lattice strips

Plastic electrical tape

Large box with crumpled papers (for positioning and soldering)

20-gauge tinned copper wire

Copper patina for solder

ASSEMBLY ITEMS

Brass lamp cap, 3 x 3 inches (7.6 x 7.6 cm) square

19-inch (48.3 cm) lamp base

Suggested finished size for each panel: 9 x 14 inches (22.8 x 35.6 cm)

8. Using both hands, grasp the four top edges of the panels and gently lift them up. Use the rulers to help hold one bottom corner in a squared position. Position the four sides so that the top edges form a square. Press the overlapping pieces of tape down firmly onto the adjacent panel to connect them. Make sure the panels are aligned correctly when you do this.

9. Flux and tack-solder the top and bottom corners with 50/50 solder at the points shown in figure 1. Tack-solder at several points along each side seam between the pieces of tape. Keep the panels square as you do this.

10. Remove a piece of tape at a time, and tack-solder each seam in these areas. Don't expect your soldering to be as neat as it would be on a flat panel. You're simply dropping solder into the slanted seams to stabilize them so that the shade will be strong enough to hold together and stand by itself.

11. Flux the top foil seam on all four panels. Shape a length of the tinned copper wire with needle-nose pliers around the top inner seam, tack-soldering as you work your way around it. Overlap the wire slightly at the end. Lightly tin the top seam and wire to stabilize the lamp's top.

12. Use a wire brush to clean the lamp cap. Apply flux to it. While holding it with a hot pad or pliers, tin the outside of the lamp cap with a slight amount of 60/40 solder. The brass will get very hot, so be careful. Allow the cap to cool, and remove the flux residue.

13. Place the cap level atop the shade so that its corners line up and the edges touch the top seams or even overlap slightly. Tack-solder the cap to the seams in as many places as possible. This will look messy, but it is a necessary step.

14. Turn the shade over. Place it in a box filled with crumpled papers to help position it so that you can work on the bottom edges.

15. Flux the bottom edges of the shade. Shape a length of the wire with needle-nose pliers around the seam. Use 50/50 solder to tack the wire flat to the seam around all four sides, overlapping the wire slightly at the end. Tin and tack-solder the edge with 50/50 solder. High-bead the edge with 60/40 solder. Clean off the flux residue.

16. With the shade still positioned upside-down in the box, flux and solder the inside edge of the lamp cap, attaching it to all inner seams and wire (photo 1).

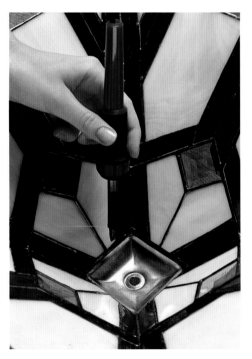

Photo 1

17. Flux and tack-solder the inside seams of the lamp in as many places as possible.

18. Take the lamp out of the box, and lay the shade on one side. High-bead the inner corner seams with 60/40 solder, turning the shade as needed. Clean off the flux residue from the inner corner seams and inside the lamp cap. Apply patina to all inner seams and around the lamp cap seam.

19. To support the shade while you finish soldering the outside seams, place it on an angle in the box with one of the outer seams in a horizontal position. Use 60/40 solder to slowly high-bead this seam. Clean off the flux residue. Repeat this process on the other three sides, turning the shade as needed. As a final step, touch up any spots on the seams with solder, then clean the shade.

20. Apply copper patina to the outer corner seams and the lamp cap.

21. Polish and place the shade on the lamp base, positioning the hole in the cap over the screw end of the lamp base top. Attach the lamp base finial to hold the lamp on the base.

Figure 1

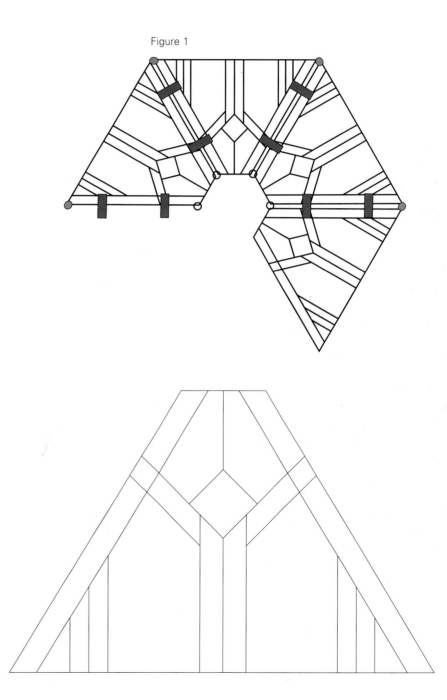

Man-in-the-Moon Nightlight

This comforting nightlight optimizes the effect of glowing light cast
on glass layers. The addition of a cast glass piece adds to the visual effect.

GLASS

Clear/iridescent

Pink and clear/rippled/cathedral

Clear/iridescent cast glass moon face (or similar round object), 4 inches (10.2 cm) in diameter

TOOLS & EQUIPMENT

Basic toolbox and supplies

Copper foil toolbox

SUPPLIES

2 feet (61 cm) of ¼-inch (.64 cm) U-channel zinc came

⁷⁄₃₂-inch (.55 cm) and ¼-inch (.64 cm) black-backed copper foil

50/50 and 60/40 solder

Black patina

ASSEMBLY ITEMS

Nightlight with electrical cord

Wooden rectangular fan-lamp base (3½ x 7½ inches [8.9 x 19.1 cm]) with 2 grooves about ¼-inch (.64 cm) wide and deep, about ½ inch (1.25 cm) apart from each other, and with 1-inch (2.5 cm) round hole drilled near the back to hold light and cord

Finished size of front lamp piece: 11 x 7½ inches (27.9 x 19.1 cm) Back piece: 9½ x 6½ inches (24.1 x 16.5 cm)

INSTRUCTIONS

1. Enlarge the two project templates (front and back) to the finished sizes indicated. Position the cast moon face or other object on the circle of the first template. Trace its outline.

2. Use the English method to cut out and number the glass pieces on top of the template. Groze and grind them to fit the template. Grind and smooth the edges of the cast glass piece.

3. Use ¼-inch (.64 cm) foil to cover the edges of the cast piece. Foil the remaining front glass pieces with the ⁷⁄₃₂-inch (.55 cm) foil. Foil the curved edge of the back piece with the same foil, overlapping the straight bottom edge slightly.

4. Position the pieces on the front template. Flux, tack-solder, and flat-fill the inner seams with 50/50 solder. High-bead the seams with 60/40 solder. Then clean off the flux residue.

5. Turn over the piece. Cradle the front of the cast glass piece in a hot pad or small towel on top of your work surface so that you can work on the back of it. Flux, flat-fill, high-bead, and clean the back, as you did the front.

6. Pick up the piece with the hot pad or towel and hold it along the straight bottom edge. Flux and high-bead the entire rounded edge with 60/40 solder. Clean off the flux residue. Set the piece aside.

7. Hold the bottom of the back piece so that you can flux and high-bead the rounded edge. Clean off the flux residue.

Photo 1

8. Cut a length of zinc came to fit the bottom edge of the back piece. Slide the piece into the came's channel on your work surface. Flux and tack-solder the bottom sides where the foil and zinc meet (photo 1).

9. Cut a second length of zinc came to fit the bottom edge of the front piece. Slide the glass edge into the channel, fitting it as tightly as possible. Hold the piece in place. Wire-brush and flux the seams where they touch the zinc. Tack-solder the seams to hold the came and glass together. Clean the flux residue, turn the piece over, and repeat this process on the other side.

10. Clean both the front and back pieces well before applying the patina. Let the patina dry.

11. Insert the electrical socket into the hole in the wooden base (see page 87). Stand the two glass panels up in the grooves.

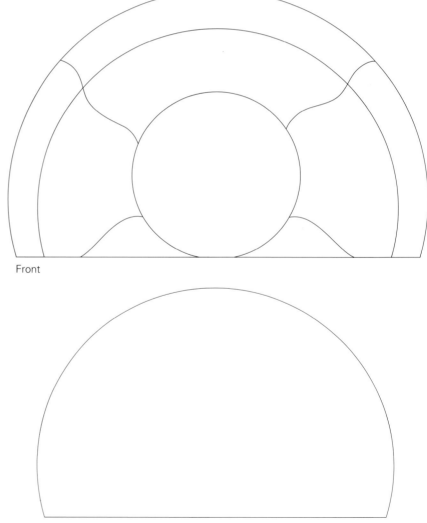

Front

Back

Mirror with Basket Design

This copper-foiled piece shows you how to combine two glass layers, a process known as plating. The small flower overlays are tacked on as a final step.

GLASS

Clear/textured
Beige/opalescent
White/opalescent
Mixed purple and
lavender/opaque
Purple/cathedral
12-inch-square (30.5 x 30.5
cm) mirror tile

TOOLS & EQUIPMENT

Basic toolbox and supplies
Copper foil toolbox

SUPPLIES

3/16-inch (.48 cm) and 7/32-inch
(.55 cm) copper foil
50/50 and 60/40 solder
Clear nail polish
Copper patina for solder
18-gauge tinned wire

Suggested finished size:
approximately 12 x 10 inches
(30.5 x 25.4 cm)

INSTRUCTIONS

1. Enlarge the project templates to the suggested finished size. Use copper foil shears to cut apart the pattern pieces. Cut and number each piece of glass for the front template showing a basket with attached flowers and the overlay flowers. Groze and grind the pieces as needed.

2. Use the back template to cut out the mirror. When grinding the mirror, be careful not to scratch the silver backing.

3. Foil the pieces in the first template, using 7/32-inch (.55 cm) foil on the larger clear textured glass and 3/16-inch (.48 cm) foil on the smaller pieces. Set aside the overlay pieces for later.

4. Position the basket and attached flowers on your template. Flux, tack-solder, and flat-fill the seams with 50/50 solder. High-bead the seams with 60/40 solder. Use a hot pad to pick up the piece at the bottom, and high-bead the top edges of the flower. When soldering, be careful to hold the project over your work surface at all times and avoid dripping any solder on your hands or arms.

5. Clean off the flux residue, turn the panel over, then flux and flat-fill the seams on the back. (Do not high-bead these seams.) Clean off the flux residue and polish the piece. Set it aside for later assembly.

6. Seal the edges of the mirror with clear nail polish to prevent chemicals from seeping between the silver backing and the glass. Let the polish dry.

7. Foil the mirror with 7/32-inch (.55 cm) foil. Position the mirror and six ribbon pieces in place according to the finished photo. Flux, tack-solder, and flat-fill the ribbon pieces to the mirror using 50/50 solder. High-bead the seams with 60/40 solder. Use a hot pad to pick up the piece at the bottom in your free hand. High-bead with 60/40 solder along the outer edge of the ribbons.

8. Clean off the flux residue, turn the panel over, and repeat the soldering on the back of the ribbons.

9. On the same side (back), lightly flux and tin the bottom edge of the foil on the mirror. Clean off the flux residue.

10. Hold the bottom of the mirror in your free hand with a hot pad. The next step is a bit tricky, so read and think about what you're going to do before you begin.

11. Unroll a length of solder wire and bend the end upward so that it is close to the edge of the ribbons. Moving back and forth from the

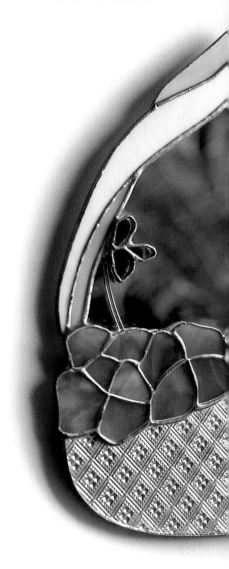

end of the solder wire to the edge, and turning the piece as the solder solidifies, high-bead the top ribbon edges. Clean off the flux residue, and polish the whole piece on the front and back. Place the piece flat on your work surface.

12. Position the assembled bottom piece on top of the mirror, aligning the edges. Lightly flux the adjoining edges, then carefully tack-solder the two seams to hold the pieces together. (Add only as much flux as necessary so that you don't trap flux residue between the two pieces.) Hold the solder wire close to the edge and very lightly coat the edges as best you can, closing up the space between the two pieces.

13. Use the hot pad to pick up the piece again, holding it so that you can access the bottom edge. Continue to lightly solder the seam until smooth, turning the piece as you go. Clean off the flux residue.

14. Lightly flux and tack-solder the seam where the flowers and the ribbons meet. Clean off the flux residue.

15. Apply copper patina to the seams with a cotton swab, working carefully to avoid getting any chemicals on the glass or mirror.

16. Position the petals for the small overlay flowers on top of the paper template. Flux, flat-fill, and high-bead the center areas. With a hot pad or needle-nose pliers, pick up each of the soldered flowers and carefully high-bead all the edges. Clean off the flux residue, and patina the front and back of each. Allow the patina to dry. Clean the glass on each well.

17. Using the template as a guide, cut three pieces of wire that match the dotted lines. Flux and solder the ends of the wires to the flowers where shown. Clean off the flux residue. Apply patina to the wires, and allow it to dry.

18. Place the flowers on the mirror in the position indicated. To protect the mirror when fluxing and soldering, slide a piece of paper underneath each flower as you work. Lightly flux and tack-solder the flowers where they touch the side ribbon pieces, where they touch each other, and the bottom ends of the wires. Carefully clean off the flux residue. Remove the paper.

19. Twist a piece of 18-gauge tinned wire into a loop to hang the mirror. On the back side of the panel, solder the ends of the loop into the existing seam and along the top of the mirror where it joins the ribbons. Clean off the flux residue.

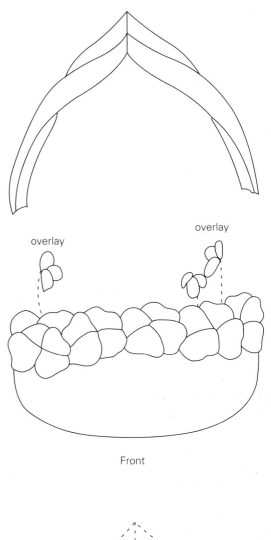

overlay   overlay

Front

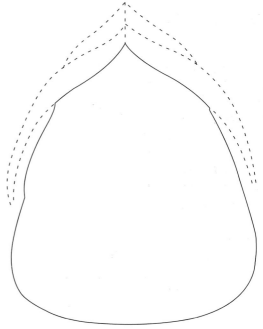

Back (mirror)

Vintage Grape Transom

This design can be sized to fit your particular window. The one shown here fits between kitchen cabinets over a sink.

GLASS

Mixed beige and white/opaque

Mixed brown/opaque

Mixed green/opaque

Mixed purple/wavy/cathedral

TOOLS & EQUIPMENT

Basic toolbox and supplies

Copper foil toolbox

SUPPLIES

4 feet (1.2 m) of ¼-inch (.64 cm) U-channel zinc came

$\frac{3}{16}$-inch (.48 cm) or $\frac{7}{32}$-inch (.55 cm) black-backed copper foil

50/50 and 60/40 solder

Black patina made for solder

Black patina made for zinc

Several brass pin backings

18-gauge tinned wire

Suggested finished size: 30 x 8 inches (76.2 x 20.3 cm)

INSTRUCTIONS

1. Enlarge the template to the suggested finished size. Trace the template onto kraft paper, and use copper foil pattern shears to cut the pieces apart. Cut and number the glass pieces, grozing and grinding them as needed to fit the pattern.

2. Apply copper foil to the pieces, and position them on the template.

3. Flux, tack-solder, and flat-fill the inner seams with 50/50 solder. High-bead the inner seams with 60/40 solder. Clean off the flux residue. Tin the bottom edge.

4. Cut one piece of zinc came to fit along the top edge and two to fit along the side edges. Use a couple of bumpers to hold the bottom foiled edge. Miter the corners at the top. Cut the ends of the side pieces at an angle to meet the curves at the bottom of the glass. Clean the came, and tack-solder the places where the foil touches it. Solder the zinc corners. Clean off the flux residue.

5. Apply black patina made for solder to the solder lines. Clean the zinc, and apply the patina made for zinc. Turn over the piece. Solder and patina the back as you did the front.

6. Invert the piece and hold it up so that you can high-bead the bottom edge where you tinned it. Clean off the flux residue, and apply black patina made for solder.

7. To make hangers for the piece that allow you to either screw the piece inside a window frame or doorway, or hang the piece from a chain, use wire cutters to clip off the pin ends of brass pin backings (photo 1).

8. Clean the zinc where you wish to attach the clips so that you can mount the piece in a window or doorway. (We suggest one at the top and bottom of both of the sides. You can bend the hangers with pliers if needed for your particular situation.) Flux and solder the clips to the zinc came. Clean off the flux residue, and apply black patina made for solder to the solder joints.

9. To simulate grape tendrils, wind two short lengths of tinned wire around a pencil to curl them. You'll attach these wires to the back of the panel at the solder seams (photo 2). Before you attach them, patina the wire, leaving about ½ inch (1.25 cm) clean on the end you want to attach.

Photo 1

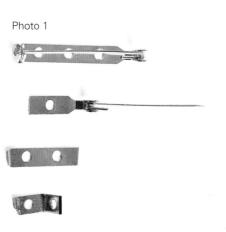

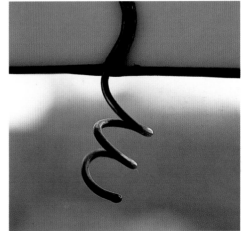

Photo 2

10. Hold each wire with needle-nose pliers, placing the clean end along the seam on the back. Apply a little flux to the solder seam, and solder the wire along the seam. Repeat this process on the other seam. Apply patina to the solder joints.

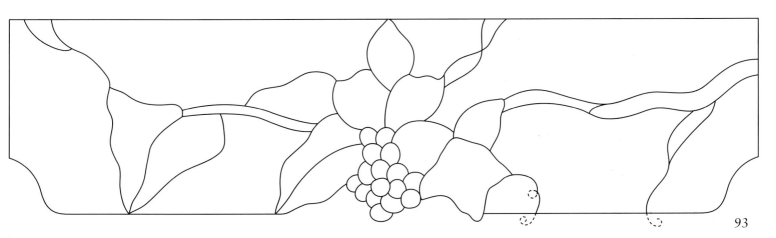

93

Floating Butterfly Panel

Open spaces in the wings of a butterfly are filled with solder and nuggets to create a jewel-like effect. Scraps of colored glass add more visual interest. Tinned wire pieces added at the end serve as decorative antennae.

GLASS

Clear/wavy

Mixed yellow and orange/opaque

Mixed teal and pink/opaque

Pink/opaque

Mixed brown/cathedral

White/wispy

4 yellow medium-sized nuggets (globs)

1 light-blue medium-sized nugget (glob)

TOOLS & EQUIPMENT

Basic toolbox and supplies

Copper foil toolbox

SUPPLIES

6 feet (1.8 m) of ¼-inch (.64 cm) U-channel zinc came

³⁄₁₆-inch (.48 cm) and ⁷⁄₃₂-inch (.55 cm) black-backed copper foil

50/50 and 60/40 solder

2 brass hangers

18-gauge tinned wire

Black patina for solder

Black patina for zinc

Black jack chain

Suggested finished size: 7½ x 32 inches (19 x 81.3 cm)

INSTRUCTIONS

1. Enlarge the template to the suggested finished size. Trace the four yellow glass nuggets on the wings of the left butterfly where shown on the template. Likewise, trace the blue nugget on the right butterfly.

2. Trace the pieces onto kraft paper, and use copper foil shears to cut the pieces apart. Cut out and number the glass pieces, grozing and grinding them to fit the pattern in preparation for copper foiling.

3. Apply copper foil to the glass pieces, overlapping the foil slightly on the outer edges that will be covered later with the zinc came frame. Position them on the template.

4. Flux and tack-solder the outer edges of the piece with 50/50 solder. Flux and flat-fill all inner seams that touch with 50/50 solder (excluding the open areas in the yellow butterfly). High-bead the seams with 60/40 solder. When high-beading, leave a small margin around the edges of the piece to allow room for the zinc frame.

5. To solder the yellow butterfly, drop 50/50 solder into the spaces between the glass pieces and nuggets. After flat-filling these areas, finish the top with a high-beaded layer of 60/40 solder. Flux as needed.

6. Use a saw to cut and miter the zinc came to fit around the piece as a frame/border. Hold the entire configuration (glass pieces and frame) in place with nails, making sure that everything fits. After this step, lift out each side of the frame to add a hanger to the top of the came. Tin the hangers, and solder them.

7. Clean each juncture of a seam with the frame before soldering it. Clean and solder the corners.

8. Clean the front of the panel thoroughly, and apply the black patina made for solder to the solder seams. Clean the zinc came, and apply the black patina made for zinc.

9. Turn over the panel, and solder the back of it as you did the front. Apply black patina, and let it dry. Turn the panel back over.

10. Polish the panel, cleaning the glass thoroughly.

11. Cut a length of tinned wire for each of the butterflies' antennae. Bend each into shape, creating a very small loop on one end with needle-nose pliers. Flux these loops, and then apply a drop of 50/50 solder to fill each hole created by a loop. Clean off the flux residue, and apply patina to the wires.

12. Use needle-nose pliers to position the wire antennae as shown. Use a small quantity of flux and tack-solder them in place to the solder seams. Clean off the flux residue.

13. Measure out a length of chain for hanging your piece. Open the link on one end, and attach it to one of the hangers. Close the link and secure it, then repeat this process on the other side.

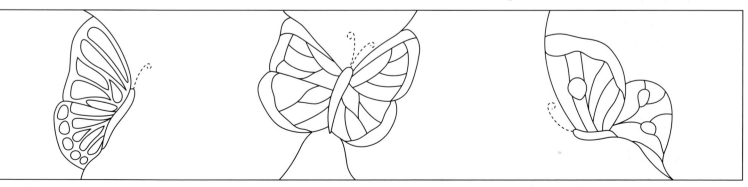

Fantasy Seascape

This copper foil project uses textured glass to represent the top of
the lighthouse. When the sun catches this bit of glass, it emulates
a beam of light. Colorful, swirled glass pieces imitate sea and sky.

GLASS

Red/cathedral

Blue/cathedral

White/streaky

Sea-green/wavy/wispy

Grey/opaque

Champagne and white/streaky

Champagne/opaque

White/opaque

TOOLS & EQUIPMENT

Basic toolbox and supplies

Copper foil toolbox

4 long wooden rulers or ¼-inch (.64 mm) lattice strips

SUPPLIES

2 lengths of ¼-inch (.64 cm) U-channel zinc came, each 6 feet (1.8 m) long

³⁄₁₆-inch (.48 cm) and ⁷⁄₃₂-inch (.55 cm) copper foil

⁵⁄₃₂-inch (.4 cm) copper reinforcing strip

50/50 and 60/40 solder

2 brass hangers

Copper patina for solder

Copper patina for zinc

White paint pen

Copper jack chain

Suggested finished size: 17 x 21 inches (43.2 x 53.3 cm)

INSTRUCTIONS

1. Enlarge the template to the suggested finished size. Trace the overall pattern, excluding the dotted-line martini glass. Trace a separate small pattern for this piece because it is an overlay that you'll add last. Use copper-foil shears to cut all the pattern pieces apart. Cut out and number the glass pieces, grozing and grinding them to fit the pattern in preparation for copper foiling. Set aside the overlay piece.

2. Apply copper foil to the glass pieces, overlapping it slightly on the edges that will be covered later with the outer zinc came frame. Position them on the template.

3. Nail the four rulers into the table around the piece to keep the sides aligned. (You'll find this helpful, since this panel is made up of so many pieces.) Insert the copper reinforcing strip between the foiled glass pieces along the horizon line of the design, bending the strip as needed. Use wire cutters to trim the copper strip exactly at each edge.

4. Flux and tack-solder the outer edges of the piece with 50/50 solder. Flux and flat-fill the inner seams with 50/50 solder, then high-bead them with 60/40 solder. When high-beading, leave a small margin around the edges of the piece to allow room for the zinc frame. When working on the horizon-line seam, solder slowly since the re-strip retains a lot of heat. When you're finished, clean off the flux residue.

5. Use a saw to cut and miter the zinc came to fit around the piece as a frame/border. As you remove each wood ruler or strip, slide and nail the appropriate came border piece into place. After this step, lift out

97

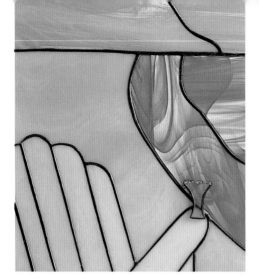

Photo 1

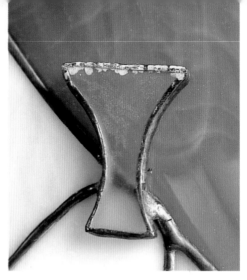

Photo 2

each side of the frame to add a hanger to the top of the came. Tin the hangers, and solder them.

6. At each corner and juncture of a seam with the frame, clean the area before soldering it.

7. Clean the front of the panel thoroughly, and apply the copper patina made for solder to the solder seams. Clean the zinc came, and apply the copper patina made for zinc.

8. Turn the panel over, and solder the back of it as you did the front. Apply patina, and let it dry. Carefully turn the panel back over.

9. Grind the overlay piece (martini glass) to fit the pattern, and apply foil to the edges. Apply a small amount of flux to the edges of the piece, and tin them with solder.

Clean off the flux residue, and apply patina to the solder. Clean the shape thoroughly.

10. On the front of the panel, position the overlay piece so that it overlaps the arm of the chair (photo 1). Using very little flux, tack-solder along each edge of the glass to the solder seams (photo 2). Clean off the flux residue.

11. Use the white paint pen to dot salt along the top edges of the glass.

12. Polish the panel, cleaning the glass thoroughly.

13. Measure out a length of chain for hanging your piece. Open the link on one end, and attach it to one of the hangers. Close the link and secure it, then repeat this process on the other side.

Perched Pelican Panel

The eye of the pelican in this design is made of a small drop of solder. The bird in the sky is created by soldering a gap between glass pieces.

GLASS

Yellow/textured/cathedral
White/wispy
Peach with white/swirled
Mixed green/cathedral
Gold with white/opaque
Small piece (scrap)
of gold/opaque
(for feet and beak)
Brown and white/opaque
Mixed green/opaque

TOOLS & EQUIPMENT

Basic toolbox and supplies
Copper foil toolbox
4 long wooden rulers or
¼-inch (.64 mm) lattice strips

SUPPLIES

2 lengths of ¼-inch (.64 cm)
U-channel zinc came,
each 6 feet (1.8 m) long
³⁄₁₆-inch (.48 cm) or ⁷⁄₃₂-inch
(.55 cm) copper foil
⁵⁄₃₂-inch (.4 cm)
copper reinforcing strip
50/50 and 60/40 solder
2 brass hangers
Copper patina for solder
Copper patina for zinc
Copper jack chain

Suggested finished size:
25 x 16 inches (63.5 x 40.6 cm)

INSTRUCTIONS

1. Enlarge the template to the suggested finished size. Trace the pieces onto kraft paper, and use copper foil pattern shears to cut them apart. Cut out and number the glass pieces, grozing and grinding them to fit the pattern in preparation for copper foiling.

2. Foil all the inside seams of the design, overlapping the foil slightly on the outer edges that will be covered later with the zinc came frame. Apply copper foil to the glass pieces, and position them on the template.

3. Nail the four rulers into the table around the piece to keep the sides aligned. Insert a length of copper reinforcing strip along the seam of the template that spans the lower edges of the clouds directly over the bird's head. Use wire cutters to cut the copper reinforcing strip exactly at each edge.

4. Flux and tack-solder the outer edges of the piece with 50/50 solder. Flux and flat-fill the inner seams that touch with 50/50 solder (excluding the gap between glass pieces that forms the bird in the sky). High-bead the seams with 60/40 solder. When high-beading, leave a small margin around the edges of the piece to allow room for the zinc frame.

5. When the seams are done, use solder to fill in the gap in the sky area that looks like a flying bird. Create a nicely rounded top. Create the eye of the pelican by dropping a bead of solder into the appropriate spot. Clean off the flux residue.

6. Use a saw to cut and miter the zinc came to fit around the piece as a frame/border. As you remove each wood ruler or strip, slide and nail the appropriate came border piece into place. After this step, lift out each side of the frame to add a hanger to the top of the came. Tin the hangers, and solder them.

7. At each corner and juncture of a seam with the frame, clean the area before soldering it.

8. Clean the front of the panel thoroughly, and apply the copper patina made for solder to the solder seams. Clean the zinc came, and apply the copper patina made for zinc.

9. Turn the panel over, and solder the back of the panel as you did the front. Apply patina, and let it dry. Turn the panel back over.

10. Polish the panel, cleaning the glass thoroughly.

11. Measure out a length of chain for hanging your piece. Open the link on one end, and attach it to one of the hangers. Close the link and secure it, then repeat this process on the other side.

Peaceful Panda Design

The nose of the panda in this design was too small to cut from glass, so we used a bit of solder instead. The two bamboo leaves that the panda appears to be eating are overlay glass pieces.

GLASS

Beige/opaque

White/opaque

White/wispy

Black/opaque

Green/wispy

Mixed purple and white/opaque

TOOLS & EQUIPMENT

Basic toolbox and supplies

Copper foil toolbox

SUPPLIES

5 feet (1.5 m) of ¼-inch U-channel zinc came

⁷⁄₃₂-inch (.55 cm) black-backed copper foil

⁷⁄₃₂-inch (.55 cm) copper foil

50/50 and 60/40 solder

2 brass hangers

Black patina for solder

Black patina for zinc

Black jack chain

Suggested finished size:
10½ x 16½ inches (26.7 x 41.9 m)

INSTRUCTIONS

1. Enlarge the template to the suggested finished size. Trace the over-all pattern on kraft paper, excluding the dotted leaves. Trace a separate small pattern for the leaves; they are overlay pieces that you'll add last. Use copper foil pattern shears to cut apart all the pattern pieces. Number and cut out the glass pieces, grozing and grinding them to fit the pattern in preparation for copper foiling.

2. Foil the white sky pieces with black-backed copper foil. Foil all other pieces with regular copper foil, overlapping slightly on the outer edges that will be covered later with the zinc came frame. Position the pieces on the template, excluding the overlay leaves.

3. Flux and tack-solder the outer edges of the piece with 50/50 solder. Flux and flat-fill all inner seams that touch with 50/50 solder (excluding the open space for the panda's nose). High-bead the seams with 60/40 solder. When high-beading, leave a small margin around the edges of the piece to allow room for the zinc frame. When the seams are done, fill in the nose with solder, creating a nicely rounded top. Clean off the flux residue.

4. Use a saw to cut and miter the zinc came to fit around the piece as a frame/border. Hold the entire configuration (glass pieces and frame) in place with nails, making sure that everything fits. After this step, lift out each side of the frame to add a hanger to the top of the came. Tin the hangers, and solder them.

5. At each corner and juncture of a seam with the frame, clean the area before soldering it. Clean off the flux residue.

6. Clean the front of the panel thoroughly, and apply the copper patina made for solder to the solder seams. Clean the zinc came, and apply the copper patina made for zinc.

7. Turn the panel over, and solder the back of the panel as you did the front. Apply patina, and let it dry. Turn the panel back over.

8. Polish the panel, cleaning the glass thoroughly.

9. Tin the overlay pieces (leaves). Clean them and then apply patina. Position them over the panda's

mouth, and apply a little flux before tack-soldering them to the adjoining mouth and hand seam. Clean off the flux residue and reapply patina where needed.

10. Measure out a length of chain for hanging your piece. Open the link on one end, and attach it to one of the hangers. Close the link and secure it, then repeat this process on the other side.

Yellow-Eyed Cat Panel

This appealing design, made with many intricate pieces, was inspired by a colorful painting. The bright eyes of the cat are amber nuggets.

GLASS

Black/opaque

White/opaque

Varied blue/opaque

Mixed gold and
orange/opaque

Light green/opaque

Small piece (scrap) of pink

2 amber nuggets (globs)

TOOLS & EQUIPMENT

Basic toolbox and supplies

Copper foil toolbox

4 long wooden rulers or
¼-inch (.64 mm) lattice strips

SUPPLIES

6 feet (1.8 m) of ⅜-inch
(.95 cm) U-channel zinc came

³⁄₁₆-inch (.48 cm) copper foil

⁷⁄₃₂-inch (.55 cm) black-backed
copper foil

50/50 and 60/40 solder

Black marking pen

Copper patina made for solder

Copper patina made for zinc

2 brass hangers

Black jack chain

Suggested finished size:
15 x 17 inches (38.1 x 43.2 cm)

INSTRUCTIONS

1. Enlarge the template to the suggested finished size, and trace the nuggets in the position of the cat's eyes. Trace the pieces onto kraft paper. Use copper foil pattern shears to cut the pattern pieces apart. Number and cut out the glass pieces. Groze and grind the glass and nuggets to fit the pattern in preparation for copper foiling.

2. Foil the glass pieces, using black-backed foil on the nuggets and white pieces, and regular foil on the rest of the pieces. Overlap the foil slightly on the outer edges that will be covered later with the zinc came frame. Position the pieces on the template.

3. Nail the four rulers into the table around the piece to keep the sides aligned.

4. Flux and tack-solder the outer edges of the piece with 50/50 solder. Flux and flat-fill the inner seams with 50/50 solder, then high-bead them with 60/40 solder. When high-beading, leave a small margin around the edges of the piece to allow room for the zinc frame. When you're finished, clean off the flux residue.

5. Use a saw to cut and miter the zinc came to fit around the piece as a frame/border. As you remove each wood ruler or strip, slide and nail the appropriate came border piece into place. After this step, lift out each side of the frame to add a hanger to the top of the came. Tin the hangers, and solder them.

6. At each corner and juncture of a seam with the frame, clean the area before soldering it. Clean off the flux residue.

7. Clean the front of the panel thoroughly, and apply the copper patina made for solder to the solder seams. Clean the zinc came, and apply the copper patina made for zinc.

8. Turn over the panel, and solder the back of the panel as you did the front. Apply patina, and let it dry. Turn the panel back over.

9. Use a permanent black marker to color the pupil of each eye.

10. Polish the panel, cleaning the glass thoroughly.

11. Measure out a length of chain for hanging your piece. Open the link on one end, and attach it to one of the hangers. Close the link and secure it, then repeat this process on the other side.

Mystical Tree Panel

Gently curved lines between nearly transparent glass are
filled with pieces of scrap lead covered with decorative soldering.
A textured, random result emulates tree branches. Overlay leaves
made of brass shim and wire are added at the end.

GLASS

Gray antique/cathedral

TOOLS & EQUIPMENT

Basic toolbox and supplies
Copper foil toolbox

SUPPLIES

6 feet (1.8 m) of 3/8-inch
(.95 cm) U-channel brass
came
Small scraps of lead came
7/32-inch (.55 cm) black-
backed copper foil
50/50 and 60/40 solder
.062-inch (1.6 mm) brass
sheeting (shim)
2 brass hangers
18-gauge tinned wire
Black patina for solder
Gold paint pen
Brass jack chain

Suggested finished size: 14 x 24
inches (35.6 x 61 cm)

INSTRUCTIONS

1. Enlarge the template to the suggested finished size. Trace the template on kraft paper, and use copper foil pattern shears to cut out the pattern pieces. Remove the tree limb pieces.

2. Number and cut out the background pieces from the glass. Groze and grind them to fit the pattern.

3. Foil the pieces with black-backed copper foil, overlapping the foil slightly on the outer edges that will be covered later with the zinc came frame. Position them on the template. The empty spaces form the branches.

4. Apply flux to any areas where the glass pieces touch (such as where the limbs narrow). Tack-solder these areas with 50/50 solder. After the pieces are tacked together, slide the template out from underneath the glass. The pieces of glass will now be on your wood work surface. When you fill the branches with lead and solder, this surface will burn slightly.

5. In the wider open areas that form the branches, place small scraps of lead to help fill in the spaces. (You'll be covering these pieces with solder.) In some curved areas, it will be possible to incorporate continuous slices of came.

6. Fluxing as you go, flat-fill the areas containing the lead pieces with 50/50 solder. Drop balls of molten solder into the spaces, dragging the iron along in short strokes to create texture. The pools of solder are hot and take time to solidify, so you'll have to work slowly. Don't worry about making the surface look perfect, the effect should be random and natural looking.

7. After soldering the larger areas, high-bead the smaller seams with 60/40 solder, creating a contrast between the bumpy texture and smooth lines. Clean off the flux residue when you're finished.

8. Use a saw to cut and miter the brass came to fit around the piece as a frame/border. Hold the entire configuration (glass pieces and frame) in place with nails, making sure that everything fits and is square. After this step, lift out each side of the frame to add a hanger to the top of the came. Tin the lower edge of the hangers, and solder them into the brass channel.

9. Clean the brass came at the corners and where the foiled seams meet it. Flux and solder the corner seams, and tack-solder the foiled pieces to the brass frame along the border. Clean off the flux residue.

10. Apply black patina to the solder lines. Use the gold paint pen to color the solder joints on the brass.

11. Turn the panel over carefully. Flux and flat-fill the seams on the back with enough 50/50 solder to cover up any exposed lead scraps. High-bead the narrow seams with 60/40 solder, as you did on the front.

12. To add the overlays, use metal shears or scissors to cut the brass shim into around 45 leaves. Wipe each leaf to clean it. Attach the leaves to the tree limbs where desired with a small amount of flux and solder. Clean off the flux residue immediately.

13. Make the small branch shoots by cutting and bending lengths of tinned wire into shape before tack-soldering one to each leaf. Arrange the shoots as you wish, and solder the free ends of the wires to the branches. Clean off the flux residue immediately.

14. Clean the brass leaves again before applying patina to the wire and solder tack-joints.

15. Clean up any areas on the glass that need it.

16. Measure out a length of chain for hanging your piece. Open the link on one end, and attach it to one of the hangers. Close the link and secure it, then repeat this process on the other side.

Nostalgic Moon & Vines Design

In this beautiful piece you'll combine small copper-foiled leaves with lead came, rendering spectacular results. A glass overlay piece in the center of the moon adds to the dimension of the piece. As an optional step, you can add a wooden frame over the zinc came frame.

GLASS

White/mottled/opaque
Black and white with clear/swirled
Black/opaque
Light gray/swirled/cathedral
Green/cathedral
Gold-pink/cathedral

TOOLS & EQUIPMENT

Basic toolbox and supplies
Copper foil toolbox
Lead toolbox

SUPPLIES

6 feet (1.8 m) of 7/32-inch (.55 cm) H-channel lead came
5 feet (1.5 m) of 3/8-inch (.95 cm) U-channel zinc came
7/32-inch (.55 cm) black-backed copper foil
50/50 and 60/40 solder
2 brass hangers
Black patina for solder
Black patina for zinc
Black jack chain

Suggested finished size: 32 x 22 inches (81.3 x 55.9 cm)

INSTRUCTIONS

1. Enlarge the template to the suggested finished size. Trace the pattern onto kraft paper. Use lead pattern shears to cut apart the main lines of the pattern, excluding the leaves. Use foil pattern shears to cut the leaves, branching out as needed with the narrower shears as you come to them. When you change shears, you'll need to remove the strip of paper left hanging from the connecting line before proceeding.

2. Trace the overlay leaves onto a separate piece of kraft paper, and cut them out with regular scissors. Cut the glass leaves, grozing and grinding them as needed to fit the pattern. Set them aside.

3. Cut out the background pieces that don't touch any of the leaves or vines. You don't need to grind the edges of these pieces, since you'll do this as you assemble the panel. Next, cut out all remaining pieces including the leaves and the adjacent background pieces. Groze and grind the background pieces and leaves in preparation for copper foiling.

4. Apply copper foil to the leaves and adjoining edges of the background pieces. Position them on the template. Apply copper foil to the overlay leaves and set them aside.

5. Begin leading at the bottom right of the piece. Work up along the right side. At the top right begin to lay the foiled leaves in place between the leaded pieces. Cut the lead to meet the ends of the leaves on the leaded vines. Use single lengths of came on the long vertical straight lines.

6. Continuing from the bottom edge of the panel, stack the pieces upward in each vertical section. Repeat the process of adding lead for the vines and inserting the foiled pieces where necessary. This may seem a bit tricky, but you'll soon see the relationship between pieces as you work. You need to make certain that any foiled piece has a matching foiled side adjacent to it so you'll be able to solder them together later. You'll notice that this method does not fit as tight as a regular leaded panel, but the solder will hold it all together later and fill in any small gaps.

7. Work up into the central section. When you get to the circular piece, wrap the piece of glass as you would a nugget.

8. When all of the pieces have been nailed into place, use a saw to cut and miter pieces of zinc came to fit around the frame. Hold the entire configuration (glass pieces and frame) in place with nails, making sure that everything fits. After this step, lift out each side of the frame to add a hanger to the top of the came. (If you plan to add a wooden frame later, skip adding the hangers.)

9. Clean the came joints, then flux and solder them with 50/50 solder. Flux any exposed foiled pieces and tack-solder them to each other and the outer edges, abutting the lead where necessary with 50/50 solder. Continue to flat-fill the copper-foiled pieces. Use 60/40 solder to high-bead the foiled areas. Clean off the flux residue.

10. Apply black patina for solder to the soldered seams.

11. Next, you'll turn the panel over to solder the back. Be especially careful when turning it over. It will be heavier and more fragile than the other projects in this book. After you solder the back, clean off the flux residue. Apply patina to the solder lines.

12. Turn the panel over again to the front side. (You'll notice how much sturdier and easier the piece is to turn over once the back is soldered.)

13. Cut off one flat side of a piece of lead came to fit the stem of the vine on the overlay template. As you do this, you'll take away the heart of the came and the other side of it, slicing lengthwise and removing the excess portion as you cut.

14. Flux the overlay leaves. Hold each with needle-nose pliers, and tin the edges with solder. Clean them, and apply black patina for solder to the edges.

15. Position the sliced section of lead and the surrounding leaves on the overlay template. Clean the lead where the leaves are to be soldered. Apply a little flux and tack-solder the leaves at points where they meet the lead. Clean off the flux residue and apply black patina to the solder joints.

16. Clean and carefully polish both the overlay piece and the circular piece of the panel (the moon). Place the overlay on top of the moon, lining up the lead ends with the leaded lines on either side. Clean the lead where it meets on each end and where the top left leaf touches the came. Lightly flux and tack-solder it well. Clean off the flux residue, and apply patina to all solder joints.

17. If you wish to add a wooden frame to the piece, as shown in the photo, do so at this point (refer to the project on page 79). If not, measure a length of chain for hanging your piece. Open the link on one end, and attach it to one of the hangers. Close the link and secure it, then repeat this process on the other side.

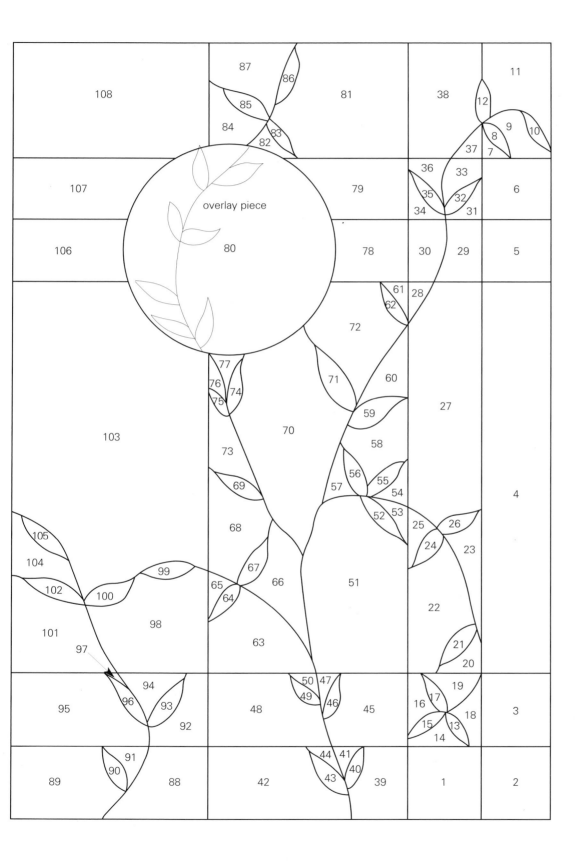

Gallery

Stained glass windows were traditionally used to admit light, add decoration, and keep out the elements. Today, glass artisans have an enormous variety of colors and textures at their disposal for creating a broad range of works—from small intimate panels for the home to large architectural installations for public enjoyment.

The following selection of images gives you a small glimpse of this very exciting and prolific field. We're grateful to these accomplished artists who allowed us to share their work. Use these inspiring pieces as a springboard for your own creative work.

Keiko Miura, Roclair Production Co., Ltd., *The New Birthright*, 1989.
46 ft. x 20 ft. 3 in. (14 x 6.2 m), dalle glass, cast glass.
Photo by Hitoshi Kawamoto

Laura Goff Parham, *Untitled*, State of the Art, Inc., Private Residence, 2001. Each panel 24 x 49 in. (61 x 124 cm), painted stained glass. Photo by Ben Parham

Left:
Alisha Volotzky,
Oceanside, 2002. 72 x 58 in. (182.8 x 197.3 cm), stained glass, steel frame, copper foil. Photo by David Kanegsberg

Right:
Alisha Volotzky,
Vicki, 2000. 77 x 58 in. (195.6 x 147.3 cm), stained glass, steel frame. Photo by Paul Moshay

Angelika Traylor,
Harmony of Heart, 2001.
18½ x 28 in.
(47 x 71.1 cm),
art glass, enameling, copper foil.
Photo by
Randall Smith

Angelika Traylor,
Autumn, 2002.
18 x 16 in.
(45.7 x 40.6 cm),
copper foiled.
Photo by
Randall Smith

Above:
Angelika Traylor, *To Florida with Love*, 2000. 32 x 20 in.
(81.3 x 50.8 cm), art glass, copper foil. Photo by Randall Smith

Upper right:
Alisha Volotzky, *Costa Mesa Round Window*, 1996. 24 in. (61 cm)
diameter, beveled leaded glass. Photo by the artist

Lower right:
Alisha Volotzky, *Annie's Bedroom Windows*, 2003.
Each 7 ft. 4 in. x 21 in. (2 m x 53.3 cm),
leaded glass, beveled, triple glazed. Photo by the artist

Top:
Conrad Schmitt Studios, Inc., *Pantocrater*, 1978.
7 x 2 ft. (210 x 61 cm). Photo by Larry Wellenstein/CSS

Bottom:
Ceilyn M. Boyd, Studio Jyoti, *Tribal Rhythms #2*, 2002. 24 x 45 in.
(61 x 114.3 cm), leaded stained glass. Photo by William A. Boyd

Above:
Cheryl Stippich, *Life Dance*, 2002.
56 x 17½ x ¼ in. (142.2 x 44.5 x .6 cm), antique jewels, bevels, glass nuggets, geode slice, mineral specimens, brass came, wave foil; copper foiled. Photo by Peter Stippich

Middle and upper right:
Cheryl Stippich, *Whirling Dervishes*, 2000.
45 x 17 x ¼ in. (114.3 x 43.2 x .6 cm), water glass, textured glass, antique jewels, mineral specimens, glass nuggets, bevels, brass wire overlay, hammered copper wire, brass filigree, decorative soldering. Photo by Peter Stippich

Lower right:
Nani Croze, Kitengela Stained Glass Studios, Ltd., *Health, Hope, and Happiness*, 2002, Aga Khan Hospital, Nairobi, Kenya. 63 x 78¾ in. (160 x 200 cm), dalle de verre, concrete, metal. Photo by Fritz Luz

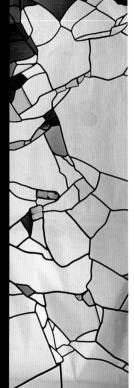

Left:
Daniel G. Wolkoff, Adams Morgan Stained Glass, *Blossoms Falling*, 2000. 68 x 20 in. (172.7 x 50.8 cm), hand-blown glass, hand-worked slab jewels, lead came. Photo by the artist

Bottom, left:
Melissa Janda, *Don't Turn Your Back on Yourself*, 2001. 6 x 11 ½ x ¼ in. (15.2 x 29.2 x .6 cm), painted and leaded glass. Photo by the artist

Bottom:
Melissa Janda, *Untitled*, 2001. 16 x 22 x ¼ in. (40.6 x 55.9 x .6 cm), painted and leaded glass. Photo by the artist

Right:
Janine S. Ody, Cristallo Architectural Glass, *Koi*, 1994. 80 x 87 x 1 ¾ in. (203.2 x 221 x 4.5 cm) mouth-blown glass, bevels, art glass, poplar; leaded. Photo by Rick Luettke

Top:
Conrad Schmitt Studios, Inc., *Joshua Tree*, 1984. 10 x 50 ft. (25.4 x 127 m), gilded calligraphy. Photo by Gordon Janowiak

Center:
Jackie Clark, *Life on the Rio Grande*, 1990, Hernandez Hall, New Mexico State University, Las Cruces. 8 x 25 ft. (2.4 x 7.6 m), mouth-blown glass, etched glass; leaded, foiled. Photo by Russ Bamert

Left:
Conrad Schmitt Studios, Inc., *Our Lady of Perpetual Help*, 2002. 5 ft. (12.7 m) diameter. Photo by Gordon Janowiak

Top and right (detail):
Jeff G. Smith,
Architectural Stained
Glass, Inc., *Hope Chapel*,
1991, Presbyterian
Healthcare Center
(Plano, Texas), Two walls:
34 x 16 ft. 7 in. (86.4 x
41.9 m), Triangle: 19 ft. 3
in. x 10 ft. 2 in. (49 x 25.5
m), mouth-blown glass,
hand-pressed lenses,
lead, solder. Photo by
Harrison Evans

Bottom left:
Keiko Miura, Roclair
Production Co., Ltd.,
Dawn, 1995. 13¾ x 98½
in. (.35 x 2.5 m), dalle
glass, molten glass.
Photo by Koji Horiuchi

Top:
Kathryn Schnabel, Studio KS,
Lord, That I May Hear My Soul, 1996. 30 x 24 in.
(76.2 x 61 cm), stained glass mosaic lightbox.
Photo by David Bentley

Bottom:
Kathryn Schnabel, Studio KS, *Grief*, 1997.
23 x 29 in. (58.4 x 73.6 cm), stained glass mosaic
framed in metal. Photo by David Bentley

Troubleshooting Tips for Stained Glass

The following tips offer you answers to frequently asked questions.

GLASS CUTTING

Why does my glass keep breaking in the wrong places?

• Make sure you're applying enough pressure on the glass cutter to make a proper score line.
• Look at the shapes you're cutting out of the glass to see if they're too difficult to cut with one score. If so, use multiple scores and breaks.
• Your glass cutter wheel might be damaged if it doesn't turn freely. Keep it lubricated and never score over a previously scored line.
• You might be working with uneven sheets of glass, such as art glass, that need to be cut on top of a soft surface such as a towel. Once the glass sheet is reduced in size, you shouldn't have a cutting problem.

SOLDERING

Why does the solder "spit" and smoke during high-beading, leaving holes and bubbles?

• Use less flux to prevent spattering.
• Completely fill in the space to prevent air pockets between foiled pieces when flat-filling the first side.

Why does the lead melt away when I solder?

• Your soldering iron is probably too hot for soldering lead. Cool the tip on a damp sponge often and consider a rheostat or controller to lower the temperature of your iron. Test it on a scrap of lead before soldering a project. Also, thin lead burns more easily than thicker lead.

Why do my copper-foiled solder lines look bumpy and dull?

• Apply less solder to the seams because too much will overfill the space on the foil and the excess will spill out.
• Use 60/40 solder when high-beading to make a shiny surface.
• Use more flux if the seams look "pitted" and rough.

Why did a piece of my glass crack during soldering?

• Glass isn't heat resistant, so if an area is heated long enough, the glass can fracture, especially on smaller pieces. The solder lines remain hot during soldering, so it's best not to overwork one area. After a couple minutes move to another area, and allow the glass and solder to cool, then go back and make any corrections. This is especially true for intricate, small pieces of a pattern and large open gaps that are filled with solder.

Why does my zinc came resist soldering, even after I've brushed and fluxed it?

• Metal came that has been allowed to oxidize won't be shiny, and wire brushing alone might not clean it enough. Use fine steel wool or another abrasive before fluxing it.
• Zinc takes more heat to solder than lead. Be sure you leave the iron on the joint long enough for the solder to melt to the zinc. A properly soldered joint won't pop apart when pulled.

COPPER FOILING

Why doesn't my foil stick well to my glass?

• Be sure your hands and the glass are clean and dry. Remove any powder that may remain from grinding. If your hands are moist, dry them, since this can also prevent the adhesive from sticking properly.
• Some silver-backed foil has a different adhesive than regular or black-backed foil and doesn't stick as well. Make sure the glass is very clean and that you crimp and/or burnish well before soldering. Once soldered, your panel will be secure.

I have trouble centering the foil on the glass pieces—help!

• Try using a tool made for foiling. Some handheld models will remove the backing and center the foil at the same time. Some free-standing models accommodate several widths of foil. Good lighting and magnifying glasses can also help with foiling.

Why are my copper-foiled pieces smaller or larger than the template after I've foiled all the pieces and laid them out?

• Maybe your pieces weren't ground exactly to fit the pattern, or you didn't use foil pattern shears. Either way, the size difference isn't important if you're making a panel that doesn't have to fit into an exact space. The outer came can be cut to any size.

LEADING

Why do my lead panels grow in size as I assemble the pieces of my project?

• The glass may not be tightly placed or seated in the grooves of the lead.

• The glass might be wider than the came channel. You can widen lead came with a plastic foil burnisher, or tap the glass into the came with the rubber side of your glazing hammer. If the glass is deeply textured, reduce the thickest part by grinding it at about a 45° angle to the bit, flattening out the peaks so that it fits better. Grinding prevents the glass from chipping if it is forced into hard came such as zinc and brass. Most came is $5/32$ inch (.48 cm), made to accommodate $1/8$-inch thick (3 mm) glass.

• If a lead piece is cut too long, it bumps the piece that follows it too far, creating loose-fitting pieces and a design larger than intended. All the cames should be cut short enough to allow abutting cames to seat completely.

• If a piece of glass just won't fit, remove the came so you can see the relationship between it and the edges of glass. You might need to groze or grind the edges again.

• When leading curvilinear glass pieces, make sure to hold the glass in one hand and shape the lead around it.

ABOUT THE AUTHOR
Christine Kellmann Stevenson

Christine Stevenson has been a professional stained glass artist since 1986. Her commercial studio in North Carolina has been open for 16 years.

Christine has reinvented herself several times throughout her career. Raised and educated in Wisconsin, she studied to become a geologist in the early 1970s. At that time, she was the only woman in her class in geological science. After completing her education, she worked for oil and gas production companies in Colorado. Later, she moved south, and earned a master's degree in educational counseling. Due to family matters, she moved to Asheville, North Carolina. The first person that she met during her move eventually became her husband.

During the 1980s, she took a stained glass course "for her sanity," and finally found her niche. For several years, she worked for a commercial studio and learned the ins and outs of the stained glass business, teaching and doing custom work. She opened her own studio in 1988.

With roots in the European tradition, but using modern tools and materials, she has created a method of teaching that works for the beginner as well as the more advanced student. Today, she teaches advanced workshops. She prefers a small studio atmosphere because she is able to retain control over all of the design and fabrication of her pieces.

Her commissioned work is found throughout the country.
Visit www.stevensonstainedglass.com to see more of her work.

Index

Index of Artists